CW01559114

WITNESSING

TO OUR

POSTMODERN

WORLD

---

*A Biblical Strategy for
the 21st Century*

By

Steve Badger

© 2003 by Steve Badger. All rights reserved.

No part of this book may be reproduced, stored in a retrieval system, or transmitted by any means, electronic, mechanical, photocopying, recording, or otherwise, without written permission from the author.

ISBN: 1-4107-1674-0 (e-book)
ISBN: 1-4107-1675-9 (Paperback)

This book is printed on acid free paper.

All Scripture quotations, unless otherwise noted, are taken from the HOLY BIBLE, NEW INTERNATIONAL VERSION ®, Copyright © 1973, 1978, 1984 by International Bible Society. Used by permission of Zondervan Publishing House. All rights reserved.

1stBooks – rev. 6/18/03

Table of Contents

Stop! Start Reading Right Here 1
Chapter 1:   The Great Western Worldview Earthquake.................. 3
Chapter 2:   If You Can't Say Anything Good… 15
Chapter 3:   Is Witnessing Optional?....................................... 23
Chapter 4:   What Do You Want Me to Say, God? 33
Chapter 5:   Put These in Your Tackle Box.............................. 41
Chapter 6:   Problems, Problems, Problems 60
Chapter 7:   Learn From Good Fishermen................................ 75
Chapter 8:   Don't You Love It When a Plan Comes Together?...... 81
Chapter 9:   No Pain, No Gain.. 99
Chapter 10: Three Encounters of the Close Kind........................ 106
Chapter 11: Don't Scare the Fish Away! 114
Chapter 12: Get Your Fishing Tackle Ready 120
Chapter 13: Let's Go Fishing! 124
Chapter 14: You Gonna Fish? Or Cut Bait?.............................. 133

Appendix
Summary of Eyre's *Dragons* 143
Cognitive Reflections of a Dissonant Gen-Xer 145
An Open Letter to My Postmodern Friends 149
Prioritize These Doctrines 158
An E-Tract on the Internet.. 159
How Can a Natural Scientist Be a Christian too?......................... 161
A Blessed Depression... 166
An Online Personal Testimony... 170
Exercises to Develop Strategy 174
Glossary 176
Useful Web Sites 179
Bibliography 180
About the Author 183

Acknowledgements

I am deeply grateful to all of my friends and colleagues who reviewed this material and offered suggestions for improvements. These include Lynn Anderson, Charlie Arsenault, LeRoy Bartel, Terry Bleek, Darwin Boston, Dale Brueggemann, Paul and Chris Drost, Calvin Johansson, James Hernando, Barbara Howard, Tom Keinath, Edgar Lawrence, Eric Lowdermilk, Wave Nunnally, Vernon Purdy, Cal Pincombe, Sharon Rooney, Bob Stallman, Rob Starner, Rich Tatum, Jim Vigil, and Jackie Dexter Welch.

I also greatly appreciate the help given by my student critics: Welbr dos Santos, Raydeen Gaddy, Dave Gross, Josh Karrer, Matthew Lindsay, Jonathan and Allison Vitale, Aaron Webster, and Chris Weinrich.

Special thanks to Pastor Brian Atkins and all my friends at Sheldon Christian Fellowship in Birmingham, England, for their insights.

Thanks, dear friends, for all of your suggestions. I apologize to you for failing, at times, to take your advice.

Any errors in fact or in logic are solely my fault and not the fault of these friends and colleagues who lent me their assistance.

Dedication

This book is dedicated to all the people who ever told me about Jesus' love for me and my need for his salvation—

And to all the people who will try to implement the ideas in this book.

Return the Cross to Golgotha

I simply argue that the cross be raised again
at the center of the marketplace
as well as on the steeple of the church.
I am recovering the claim that Jesus was not crucified
in a cathedral between two candles;
But on a cross between two thieves: on a town garbage heap;
at a crossroad of politics so cosmopolitan that they had to write
His title in Hebrew and in Latin and in Greek.
And at the kind of place where cynics talk smut,
and thieves curse and soldiers gamble.
Because that is where He died, and that is what He died about.
And that is where Christ's men ought to be,
and what church people ought to be about.

—Source unknown

Explanatory Notes

The text in this book is set in several different styles. Ordinary text looks like this. The first time a technical word is used, the word is set in SMALL UPPERCASE LETTERS and a brief definition is included in the glossary in the appendix.

> 📖 Most long quotations look like this, indented with vertical lines on the right and left. Some very short quotations are just placed in quotes and left in the ordinary text.

✝ *Scripture quotations that quote Jesus appear like this.*

🕊 *Almost all other Bible quotations look like this. If just a word or phrase is quoted, it is usually left in the text and placed inside quotation marks.*

> ✎ This book is designed to be interactive. If possible, dialogue with other Christians about the ideas presented here. Suggestions for interaction are enclosed in a box like this. In order to get the most from this book, get a notebook, and when you see a box like this, write a journal of your thoughts and reactions. Writing chapter numbers by your notes will help you identify them later.

Finally, several references are made to articles found on the Internet. Be aware that the Internet is extremely dynamic—information found at a particular site today may not be there tomorrow. I have paper and electronic copies of all Internet articles that I've referenced.

Of making many books there is no end...
Ecclesiastes 12:12

Stop! Start Reading Right Here

Please don't skip the first two chapters of this book. They may be a little difficult for some readers, but you cannot fully appreciate the conclusions concerning witnessing suggested in this book until you understand the ideas presented in these two chapters.

This book is not an exhaustive, last word on postmodernism or on witnessing. I do not attempt to cover every related topic. For example, I hardly touch on the importance of the corporate church being a witness to the community in areas like fighting for justice and being the champion of those who cannot defend themselves (e.g., orphans, the unborn, widows, and the poor). I wrote it specifically with college students (all Christians should be students) and other young Christians in mind, but adults of any age should find it useful.

This book is based on four premises. The **first** is that every Christian can and should be a witness. In fact, every Christian *is* a witness—the only question is "To what are you witnessing?" Are you a witness to a living, all-powerful Savior, or to a dead, powerless religion?

The **second premise** is that we Western Christians are in a culture war—and we are losing. For the past 25-50 years our culture has been undergoing drastic changes that have made the Christian faith less and less credible to Westerners—especially the younger generations. Christianity is not even plausible to many folks, let alone credible. To make matters worse, many people (and institutions) who have embraced an anti-Christian philosophy and worldview are eager to further marginalize Christians.

The **third premise** is that far too many Christians are unaware of this culture war and unprepared to face the challenges this war poses for witnessing in the new millennium.

The **fourth premise** is that, for most Christians, the best strategy—the biblical strategy—to winning the lost is through Christians establishing significant relationships with lost people so that they can see and hear what God is doing in your life.

1

This book is designed to be interactive, not just a textbook to read. Your interactions with the pieces in the Appendix are a vital part of this book. Please read them when the text directs you to them.

You'll gain more from this book if you read part of it and then stop and reflect on what you've read. A small group with a discussion leader would be even more beneficial.

If you see some words that are new to you, use a dictionary or the Glossary in the Appendix to expand your vocabulary—we are all learners, after all!

In order to gain the most from this book, you should keep a journal and interact with the questions in each chapter. One way to do this is to buy an inexpensive composition notebook and write your thoughts and questions in it. If you have never kept a journal, I challenge you to try it and discover how rewarding it can be.

What qualifies me to write this book? That's a fair question. I have been a Christian for over 30 years, and for most of that time, active in Kingdom work. My seminary education, my pastoral experiences, the books I've read, and the witnessing classes I've attended did not do as much, however, to equip me to write this, as did my personal experiences in witnessing, including street-witnessing. I do not claim to be an expert on personal witnessing, but I do hope I am still learning. Also, I've sought the counsel of several trusted Christian leaders and scholars.

You are about to embark on an adventure that should change your Christian life. Expect some apprehension. Pray for wisdom and courage. Attempt the impossible. And be prepared to see what God's Spirit can do in the life of one person willing to pay the price of obedience. Accept the challenge of missionary William Carey: "Attempt great things for God. Expect great things from God."

I felt the Holy Spirit urging me to write this—unlike any other urging I've experienced in the past. May God extend that sense of urgency to you, too, as you prepare to engage postmodernists on what is often hostile turf.

May God be glorified and the Church enlarged in our attempts to bring people to a saving relationship with Jesus. Let it be so in my life, Lord. Amen.

Steve Badger
Springfield, Missouri
January 2003

There is nothing new under the sun...
Ecclesiastes 1:9

Chapter 1
The Great Western Worldview Earthquake

Worldviews in collision

Whether you know it or not, you have a WORLDVIEW[1]—and it plays a crucial role in determining how you understand almost everything in the world around you. What's a worldview? Russ Bush describes it as a person's basic, comprehensive understanding of reality. It includes the assumptions that you use to categorize ideas, order your thoughts, and react to experiences.[2] Thus, your worldview provides the framework that you use to help you interpret reality. Albert Wolters described worldview with these words:

- 📖 the comprehensive framework of one's basic beliefs about things.
- 📖 functions as a guide to life.
- 📖 the shared everyday experience of humankind.
- 📖 an inescapable component of all human knowing.[3]

First your family, then your CULTURE, usually shapes and forms your worldview. But when we become Christians, we should learn to allow the Bible to reshape our worldview. Over the past few centuries, the typical Western worldview has become less and less biblical to the point of completely denying even the existence of the God of the Bible. So Christians find our worldview in collision with that of most non-Christians in our culture—the very people we want to bring to faith in the Lord.

Developing a biblical worldview is crucial to living a consistent Christian life. Having a schizoid worldview—part biblical, part cultural—will retard your faith walk and make you more vulnerable to being led astray in DOCTRINE and in practice.

---

[1] Words in small uppercase letters are defined in the Glossary in the Appendix.

[2] L. Russ Bush, *A Handbook for Christian Philosophy,* Zondervan, 1991, p.322.

[3] Albert Wolters, *Creation Regained,* Eerdmans, 1985, pp.2, 4, 9.

A culture in transition

If you have ever had friends from a different culture, you know how important it is to understand their culture. This is also true if you want to be friends with people in your own culture. The difference is that you supposedly already know and understand your own culture. But perhaps you don't understand it as well as you think you do.

I was born just as World War II came to an end and grew up in the '50s and '60s. The world I live in now is not the world of my childhood and early adulthood. People think radically differently today. Dennis McCallum describes it this way:

📖 Until recently, the consensus in secular (non-Christian) thought has been *modernism*. Modernists view the world, including humans, as one gigantic machine, placing their faith in rationality (the ability of humans to understand their world), EMPIRICISM (the belief that knowledge can only be gained through our senses) and in the application of rationality and empiricism through SCIENCE and technology. Make no mistake, the modern worldview continues to exert great influence on contemporary culture.[4]

MODERNISM dominated Western culture (some say) for about 200 years—from about 1789 (on Bastille Day) to about 1989 (with the fall of the Berlin Wall). Modernism resulted from THE ENLIGHTENMENT with its excessive confidence in human reason. For the last 25 to 50 years we have been in a transition from modernism to what is most often called POSTMODERNISM, which is rapidly becoming the prevailing Western worldview. Of course, this transition has been very gradual, it is incomplete, and it is still ongoing. Its characteristics and relationship to modernism are a matter of some debate.

Before describing postmodernism, let me provide a fuller description of modernism. J. P. Moreland described modernism as a secular approach based on the autonomy of human reason. It embraces the correspondence theory of truth (that is, truth corresponds to the way things are). Modernism typically argued that the physical world is all there is and functions mechanically; thus, the scientific method is the only source of genuine knowledge (a view called scientific naturalism).[5] Modernism's recognition of the

---

[4] Dennis McCallum, "Are We Ready?" In *The Death of Truth*. Bethany House, 1996, p.13.

[5] J. P. Moreland, lectures to students at Central Bible College, March 22-23, 1999.

4

existence of ultimate truth was advantageous to Christianity, but its rejection of God prevented it from finding that truth.

James Emery White argues that the APOLOGETIC used for modernists must be completely revised to reach today's postmodern Westerners. He claims that the modernist's question "Is there a God?" has been replaced by the postmodernist's "Which God?" Modernism's question "Was Jesus the Son of God?" has become "How can I believe there's just one way to heaven?" Postmodernists do not merely ask "Is the Bible true?" but ask "Is there truth?"[6]

Whereas modernism questioned what truth is, postmodernism questions the very existence of any truth. The RELATIVISM of my youth has become the hyper-relativism of today. In 1994, Christian pollster George Barna described it this way:

> 📖 This year's research confirms that things are *not* moving toward a more conservative, biblical perspective on truth and morality. We found, for instance, that nearly three-quarters of all adults (72%) agreed that "there is no such thing as absolute truth; two people could define truth in totally conflicting ways, but both could still be correct." This is actually a larger proportion of adults who embrace this outlook than was the case just three years ago, when 67% concurred with the statement tested.[7]

Barna observed that both men and women are embracing relativism, and older Americans are too. To make matters even worse, Americans apply relativism to questions of ETHICS and morality. In this same survey, 71% of the participants agreed that there are no absolute standards of what is right and wrong that apply in all situations to everyone.[8]

Although there are many minor differences, I have found that this is also mostly true of other Westerners (e.g., the British). D. A. Carson writes that European and North American postmodernism are not precisely identical, and postmodernism within individual European countries also has several variations.[9] A church group in

---

[6] James Emery White, "Evangelism in a Postmodern World," in *The Challenge of Postmodernism*. David S. Dockery, ed. Baker, 1995, p.369.

[7] George Barna, *Virtual America*. Regal Books, 1994, pp.81, 83.

[8] Barna, p.84.

[9] D. A. Carson, *The Gagging of God*. Zondervan, 1996, p.493.

Birmingham, England affirmed much of the material in this book as equally applicable to their culture.

My local newspaper recently published an editorial by a religious studies university professor that is typical of postmodern relativism. He wrote:

> 📖 The religion of any people is actually shaped by the social conditions under which we live. In other words, the Gods [sic] we worship and what we regard as true religion depends largely on when and where we were born. Or, put another way, true religion is whatever my own personal confession happens to be.[10]

A few months later this newspaper printed another editorial written by another religious studies professor at the same university. This professor warns the reader "that any religion without critical thought tends to ultimately believe itself," he continues by saying that if this happens, "it erroneously concludes that it has unlimited access to absolute truth." He writes:

> 📖 If we have a tendency to feel secure in our religion, we may be on the dangerous verge of claiming absolute truth. If we read Crossan's book, it may help us get back on track with our lifetime journey to immortality with all the rest of the world's religious adherents.[11]

What makes absolute truth dangerous? He tells us in another editorial that the "process of learning cannot be engaged in unless one can hold that truth is plural...and that no one possesses absolute truth."[12]

Is the denial of absolute truth dangerous? Without a doubt it is if the Gospel of Christ Jesus is true! But what effect do these editorials have on readers who do not recognize these ideas as fitting the criteria that Paul gave to his readers in Colossians 2:8?

> 🕊 *See to it that no one takes you captive through hollow and deceptive philosophy, which depends on human tradition and the basic principles of this world rather than on Christ.[13]*

---

[10] Charles W. Hedrick, "True Religion? It All Depends." *Springfield News-Leader.* July 10, 2000, p.8A.

[11] Mark Boyer, "Security Holds Its Own Dangers," October 30, 2000, *Springfield News-Leader*, p.8A.

[12] Mark Boyer, "In the Bible, Truth is Plural," February 12, 2001, *Springfield News-Leader*, p.8A.

[13] Unless otherwise stated, all Scripture quotations are from the *New International Version*.

Postmodernism fits this warning perfectly. If you doubt it, open your Bible and read this verse in its context.

Postmodernism is not confined to an academic or an intellectual elite! It is part and parcel of "the earthy realities of everyday life, to what people actually do at home, at work, at play."[14] It has affected law, literature, psychology, history, all levels of education, media, arts and entertainment, and popular culture—and it now permeates religion including Christianity. The several examples repeated in this book that are quoted from editorials in my local newspaper illustrate how widespread postmodernism is.

It is such a large part of the "spirit of the age" that many apologists claim Christians cannot hope to effectively witness to most Westerners if we fail to understand postmodernism and prepare ourselves to answer many of its positions. This problem is the *raison d'être* of this book.

A comparison and description

Gene Veith compares modernism to postmodernism like this:

Modernists ..	Postmodernists...
valued unity	value diversity
looked for universal frame-works of knowledge	question all "totalizing" or "foundational" systems (METANARRATIVES)
emphasized the individual	emphasize the culture
sought order	Prize disorder

---

[14] David Lyon, "Modern and Postmodern Culture." In Christopher Partridge, ed., *Dictionary of Contemporary Religion in the Western World.* IVP, 2002.

Modernists...	Postmodernists...
valued science as a means of finding knowledge about nature	care little for scientific knowledge, but they love technology. Oblivious to how or why it works, postmodernists and the new information technologies feed on each other. Television, with its fragmented sequence of images and entertainment mentality, and computer networks, with their decentralized anarchy and their "virtual reality" fantasy worlds, practically define the postmodernist state of mind. For postmodernists, all reality is virtual reality.[15]

Modernism called for a tolerance that basically said, "Live and let live." The tolerance of postmodernism, on the other hand, insists that no one can make an exclusive claim to truth since there is no such thing as absolute truth. And so postmodernists themselves are intolerant only of us "intolerant" Christians.

Other hallmarks of postmodernism include an emphasis on:

- Individual freedom
- Mystery, that is, violations of the LAW OF NON-CONTRADICTION, do not present problems that must be solved
- A low value placed on human life (e.g., abortion, euthanasia)
- A high value placed on all other animal life (not only endangered species)
- Relationships and feelings as more important than reason and logic[16]
- Politically correct language
- The reader/interpreter of a given text creates the meaning (so we have a feminist history, Marxist history, etc.)
- The rejection of metanarratives (which are seen as a mask for a power play)
- "A precommitment to relativism or PLURALISM in relation to questions of truth."[17]

---

[15] Gene E. Veith, "Postmodern Times: Facing a World of New Challenges & Opportunities." *Modern Reformation.* Sept/Oct 1995. Found at www.capo.org/premise/95/sep/p950807.html.

[16] Kevin G. Ford, *Jesus for a New Generation.* InterVarsity Press, 1995, p.115.

[17] Much of this description is based on Alister E. McGrath's *Intellectuals Don't Need God and Other Modern Myths* (Zondervan, 1993), pp.175-181.

Jon Hinkson and Greg Ganssle summarized the contrast between postmodern thought and Christianity like this:

> 📖 Central to the postmodern structures of thought is the inadmissibility of any universal claim that is applicable and binding on all everywhere. While one is welcome to tell one's own story it may only be personal or parochial, never complete or cosmic in its sweep. Any such totalizing account is dismissed as totalitarian and taboo or, for those who follow Rorty, naive. But the Gospel is a story that is universal in its claims. It calls "all people everywhere to repent." (Acts 17:30) It is the ultimate metanarrative declared to a culture incredulous of metanarratives. Thus the universal claims of Christianity typically register as irritating atavisms of enlightenment hubris.[18] And so the Gospel is often rejected simply because it claims to be true, not because it has been examined and found to be false.[19]

"The centerpiece of the postmodern era," according to Kevin Ford, is DECONSTRUCTION.[20] This technical term requires some explanation. Deconstructionism is the child of French philosopher Jacques Derrida who proposed it for literature. Richard Rorty, Michel Foucault, and Ferdinand de Saussure developed it further. Ford describes the essential principles of deconstruction like this:

1. Objective reality does not exist, only the reality created by our minds and language. "Thus any text is made up of words whose meaning is indeterminate and whose content is not objectively verifiable."[21]

2. Our Western modern thought has embraced a "framework of polar oppositions, such as GOOD-evil, TRUTH-falsehood, MALE-female, [and] POSITIVE-negative," among others. Derrida contended Westerners "use language to create destructive, oppressive hierarchies."[22] So, they argue, language is used to suppress and

---

[18] Let me translate their phrase "irritating atavisms of enlightenment hubris." They mean that the gospel irritates postmodernists because (to them) we Christians appear prideful, arrogant, and archaic—since we still accept the Enlightenment idea that there are some universal truths.

[19] Jon Hinkson and Greg Ganssle, "Epistemology at the Core of Postmodernism: Rorty, Foucault, and the Gospel." In D. A. Carson, ed., *Telling the Truth.* Zondervan, 2000, p.85.

[20] Kevin G. Ford, *Jesus for a New Generation.* InterVarsity Press, 1995, p.119.

[21] Ford, p.120.

[22] Ford, p.120.

repress women and ethnic minorities—indeed, anyone not in power.

In his glossary, Dennis McCallum defines deconstruction as:

📖 The postmodern literary discipline of uncovering the opposing ideas implied in a text and demonstrating how the author has favored one side over the other because of his or her social context. Demonstrating how texts' truth claims defeat themselves.[23]

Deconstructionism brings to my mind a converse example from *Alice in Wonderland.* Notice how Alice responded to Humpty Dumpty when he said:

📖 "There's glory for you!"

📖 "I don't know what you mean by 'glory,'" Alice said.

📖 Humpty Dumpty smiled contemptuously. "Of course you don't—till I tell you. I meant 'there's a nice knock-down argument for you!'"

📖 "'But 'glory' doesn't mean a nice knock-down argument," Alice objected.

📖 "When I use a word," Humpty Dumpty said in a rather a scornful tone, "it means just what I choose it to mean—neither more nor less."

📖 "The question is," said Alice, "whether you can make words mean so many different things."

📖 "The question is," said Humpty Dumpty, "which is to be master—that's all."[24]

Humpty Dumpty thought the speaker (writer) should have complete control over the meaning of a word (text). Postmodernists think the meaning is beyond recovery, but probably means something different than, often the opposite of, the plain meaning.

> 🖊 Who or what do you think should be the controlling factor in what a text should mean? The reader or the author? Why? Have you ever written anything that was misinterpreted?[25]

Ford offers as an illustration the way journalism has changed in the last few decades. At one time the opinions of the journalists were

---

[23] Quoted from the glossary (p.281) of McCallum's *The Death of Truth.*

[24] Lewis Carroll, *The Annotated Alice: Alice's Adventures in Wonderland & Through the Looking Glass.* Bramhall House, 1960, pp.268-269.

[25] To get the most out of this book, keep a journal of your reactions to questions and comments enclosed in boxes like this.

reserved for the editorial page; news stories contained only the facts and the comments of the eyewitnesses. Today the opinions of the journalists are often woven right into the news account.[26]

Do you see how deconstruction erodes the historical Christian faith based on the meaning of the Bible if "you are free to find your meaning, and I am free to find mine"? Isn't it more important to try to discover what the original human author and God meant? The HERMENEUTICAL approach of postmodernists threatens not only biblical Christianity, but it also threatens to destroy the constitutional and legal foundations of many great nations.

Postmodernism encourages COGNITIVE DISSONANCE and style over substance. One example of this is Christians who are willing to tolerate mutually contradictory doctrines—or at least practices that are inconsistent with clear biblical teachings. Another example might be church members who do not care if the content of a sermon is extra-biblical as long as the delivery is interesting—or, better yet, exciting. Often our church music meets these characteristics too. These characteristics were common under modernism, but they have been multiplied and intensified by postmodernism.

Veith continues his description of the state of the culture this way:

> In a relativistic climate, the only remaining virtue is tolerance. The only philosophies that are wrong are those that believe in truth; the only sinners are those who still believe there is such a thing as sin.[27]

So in the eyes of postmodernists, we intolerant, exclusive Christians are the "sinners."

If you witness to the lordship of Christ Jesus to a postmodernist, you had better be prepared for an assertion that all religions are true. Can the postmodernists possibly be right? Is it possible that all religions are true? Philosopher Dallas Roark once told a group of college students that it is much more likely that all religions are false than that all religions are true.[28] All religions cannot possibly be true since some of them make mutually contradictory claims—unless, of

---

[26] Kevin G. Ford, *Jesus for a New Generation.* InterVarsity Press, 1995, p.121.

[27] Veith, "Postmodern Times: Facing a World of New Challenges & Opportunities."

[28] Dallas Roark (Emporia State University), Central Bible College, March 23, 2000. He is the author of *The Christian Faith, Dietrich Bonhoeffer,* and *An Introduction to Philosophy.*

course, you accept the idea that mutually contradictory propositions can both be true (violating the law of non-contradiction).

Should we be surprised that there is only one true religion and many false religions? Dr. J. Budziszewski (University of Texas at Austin) explains it this way:

> 📖 If only one religion is right, why are there so many others? I answer: Why not? There are more wrong answers than right ones to every question. What is two plus two? There is only one right answer, but there is an infinity of wrong ones. Besides, in religion we often prefer the wrong answers. If we don't want God most of all—if we want something else even more than God—then we convince ourselves that this Something Else is God, and that God isn't God after all.[29]

> ✎ How have you observed postmodernism in the world, in education, and in the church? Write your notes in your journal.

Why are you telling me?

Regardless of your age or whether you have been most influenced by modernism or postmodernism, all Christians need to understand both worldviews and how to witness to people who embrace either one.

Our culture has not completely made the transition; many are still committed to modernism. Even younger people have at least a few modernist traits.

Many of your pastors, your Sunday school teachers, and your college professors were indoctrinated in the modernist worldview. They taught you from that perspective. Much of what you learned about the Christian faith, the church, the Bible, and evangelism you learned from people who have been strongly influenced by modernism. So some of your thinking is probably from that perspective. And a modernist strategy works poorly, if at all, today when witnessing to people who embrace a postmodernist worldview.

The pendulum is rapidly swinging from modernity to postmodernity, but one day our culture is likely to swing back (or in yet another direction). Christians should be involved in determining where this pendulum swings next. And knowing where the pendulum

---

[29] J. Budziszewski, "Ask Theophilus: Too Many Religions," www.boundless.org/2000/departments/theophilus/a0000297.html.

has been will help us understand where it should go and how to get it there.

Far too many college students and graduates—including those at Christian colleges—have been so thoroughly indoctrinated with postmodernism that they fail to see the dangers to their faith. A former student told me of a recent honors graduate from a Christian college who saw no contradiction between her Christianity and her conception of postmodernism.

I think that postmodernism has taken another toll on some Christians. Many Christian students today are unwilling to pay the price in hard work to excel academically. How has postmodernism affected them academically? Total individual freedom means I am free to choose what I want to learn. Relativism means the grade a professor gives me in a course has no meaning. I can grade the professor too. And pluralism means I am free to embrace whatever "truth" I wish and still call myself a Christian.

At times students conclude that they know more about what they should and should not read or study in a course than the professor knows. I recall a student at a Christian college taking a biology course who criticized an assignment to read a book titled *How to Think about Evolution and Other Bible Science Controversies* as irrelevant.[30] I could not decide if he did not understand the meaning of the word irrelevant, or if he did not understand even the book's title. In either case, he was sure he knew more than the professor about what students in that course at that college should and should not read.

Thus some students fail to prepare to be the very best that they can be. This is true not only for many students who are preparing for ministry, but for many Christian students preparing for other professions too. I hold the postmodernist worldview partly responsible for this lack of interest in academic excellence.

🖉 How do you see yourself? As a modernist? A postmodernist? A mixture of both? Were you the same before you were a Christian as you are now? Do you think your thinking is untainted by postmodernism? What about your Christian friends?

Postmodernism has also influenced approaches to child-rearing. Priority is placed on the child's freedom to choose what is best, and

---

[30] Duane Thurman, *How to Think about Evolution and Other Bible Science Controversies.* InterVarsity Press, 1977.

any attempt to provide structure for the child is viewed as totalitarian. Instead, parents let them discover attitudes and behaviors that are personally productive to them. This approach has been common in many public schools.

Postmodernism pushes people to PRAGMATISM. This is embodied in the popular idea that if something is successful it must be "right" or "true." This was popularized in the proverb "You can't argue with success." This is true only if there are no absolute truths, and all truth is relative. This pragmatism has invaded the Christian mindset and the teaching and practices of today's churches—to our great detriment!

> ✐ In 1987 InterVarsity Press published Stephen Eyre's book *Defeating the Dragons of the World*. In it Eyre described six unbiblical values (dragons) that are so much a part of Western culture that they permeate the Church—to our great loss. A summary of his book is found in the Appendix (page 143). Eyre's portrayal of these values describes how these values fostered the transition from modernism to postmodernism. Write down all of your own reflections and observations in your journal.

There is nothing new under the sun...
Ecclesiastes 1:9

Chapter 2
If You Can't Say Anything Good...

Critique of postmodernism

Postmodernism offers no answers to humankind's problems—instead, it only tears apart the answers offered by everyone else, especially biblical answers. Paul warned his readers not to embrace false philosophies.

> *See to it that no one takes you captive through hollow and deceptive philosophy, which depends on human tradition and the basic principles of this world rather than on Christ. (Colossians 2:8)*

Paul defined a false philosophy as any philosophy that denies Christ.

Modernism was not all good, and postmodernism is not all bad. We have exchanged one set of problems for another set. How can a Christian respond to postmodernism with an effective witness? We certainly must be prepared to demonstrate its inadequacies and—whenever possible—use it to our advantage.

Those who accept the New Testament as an accurate presentation of the teachings of Jesus must respond to the challenge to the existence of absolute truth. Jesus claimed to be the Truth (John 14:6), and in his prayer for his followers, he said:

> ✝ *"Sanctify them by the truth; your word is truth." (John 17:17)*

If God is the person the Bible presents and the Bible is God's Word, we can come to no other conclusion but the Bible contains absolute truth. We have Jesus' word on it.

Daniel Taylor challenges the postmodernist criticism of believers as intolerant:

> 📖 A challenge for those who prize tolerance as one of the highest public goods is to distinguish between healthy tolerance and a diseased moral passivity or indifference. What is the difference

> between a genuinely tolerant society and a morally bankrupt one, incapable of calling evil for what it is? Is Chesterton on to something when he says tolerance is the virtue of those who don't believe in anything? Too much of what passes as tolerance in America is not the result of principled judgment but is simple moral indifference. Invoking "it's not my business" may keep us from becoming a nation of prudish snoops, but historically, it also has led nations into collaboration with great evil.[31]

Postmodernists, Taylor observes, will typically label you as intolerant just because you disagree with them on "certain hot-button topics"— all the while ignoring the same kind of intolerance toward Christians.[32] But a moral person cannot tolerate everything!

J. P. Moreland suggests that since postmodern writers use reason to argue against the validity of reason, their arguments are self-refuting.[33] In his *The Death of Truth Group Study Guide*, Dennis McCallum tells his readers to imagine this discussion:

- "There is no such thing as truth."
- "Really, is that true?"
- "Yes it is."
- "Well if that's true than there's at least one true thing—your statement! So that means it's not true that there's no such thing as truth."
- "But my statement is that there is no such thing as truth."
- "Okay, but then your statement isn't true, is it?"[34]

Do you see what self-refuting means?

How do we use these arguments when we are discussing the issues with postmodernists? Perhaps most often the dialogue will have to be extended over a long period of time, giving your friends time for reflection and the Holy Spirit time to work in their minds and hearts.

If all truth claims are valid (as postmodernism asserts), then Christianity has as much right as any to be heard and considered as valid. But many postmodernists deny us this right.

---

[31] Daniel Taylor, "Are You Tolerant? Should You Be?" *Christianity Today*. January 11, 1999, pp.42-43.

[32] Taylor, p.46.

[33] J. P. Moreland, lectures to students at Central Bible College, March 22-23, 1999.

[34] "*The Death of Truth* Group Study Guide," www.xenos.org/ministries/crossroads/dotstds.htm.

Relationship with God and an acceptance of his Word provide the only ultimate grounds on which absolute truth and moral values can be based. Without God's absolute truth, morality is merely based on community standards. And those in power or control of the community define and determine those standards. So, in the final analysis, "might makes right" for the postmodernist.

How do we know that torturing babies is wrong? How do we know that helping a sick person is right? Some non-Christians suggest that we can have a morality based on something else, but all these approaches end in failure.

> ✏ Years ago people quoted this proverb: "A person with an *experience* is never at the mercy of a person with an *argument.*" Do you think this statement true? Explain your conclusions. Write your thoughts down in your journal. We address this again in a later chapter.

How should Christians respond to the charge of intolerance? In what way can a Christian dialogue with a non-Christian? D. A. Carson offers these suggestions:

- 📖 Similarly, there can be no objection to "dialogue" as opposed to "monologue": that is, two or more people can talk together, and such talk may be the vehicle for the proclamation of the Gospel.

- 📖 But many voices advocating dialogue go much farther. In our pluralistic environment, they start to insist that dialogue between, say, a Christian and a Muslim must be so evenhanded, so open-ended, that the Christian, far from entering the discussion with an "arrogant" assumption that Christians have the "right" answer, assumes nothing, and accords opposing opinions the same authority as Christian opinions.

- 📖 Certainly opposing voices should be accorded the same *courtesy.* But if we insist that they be accorded the same *authority,* we are implicitly adopting philosophical pluralism, at the cost of affirming biblical Christianity. Although various people in the New Testament engage in dialogue (e.g., Paul reasons with people, Acts 17:2), they never do so except from a position of equivocal confidence in the truthfulness and exclusive saving power of the gospel message to which they bear witness.[35]

---

[35] Carson, *The Gagging of God.* p. 508.

Christians then must be careful to be courteous and treat those with whom we disagree with respect. But we must not—we cannot—pretend that other texts have the authority of the Scriptures.

Is communication possible among people with different worldviews? Or are different worldviews INCOMMENSURABLE? Carson provides us with a revealing experience. I realize the following quotation is a little long, but it's well worth reading!

> 📖 A few years ago I was teaching an evening course on HERMENEUTICS, a course jointly offered by several of the seminaries in the Chicago area. Not very successfully, I was trying to set out both what could be learned from the new hermeneutic, and where the discipline was likely to lead one astray. In particular, I was insisting that true knowledge is possible, even to finite, culture-bound creatures. A doctoral student from another seminary waited patiently through two or three hours of lectures, and then quietly protested that she did not think I was escaping from the dreaded positivism of the nineteenth century. Deeper appreciation for the ambiguities of language, the limits of our understanding, the uniqueness of each individual, and the social nature of knowledge would surely drive me to a more positive assessment of the new hermeneutic. I tried to defend my position, but I was quite unable to persuade her.

> 📖 Finally, in a moment of sheer intellectual perversity on my part, I joyfully exclaimed, "Ah, now I think I see what you are saying. You are using delicious irony to affirm objectivity of truth." The lady was not amused. "That is exactly what I am *not* saying," she protested with some heat, and she laid out her position again. I clasped my hands in enthusiasm and told her how delighted I was to find someone using irony so cleverly in order to affirm the possibility of objective knowledge. Her answer was more heated, but along the same lines as her first reply. I believe she also accused me of twisting what she was saying. I told her I thought it was marvelous that she should add emotion to her irony, all to the purpose of exposing the futility of extreme relativism, thereby affirming truth's objectivity. Not surprisingly, she exploded in real anger, and accused me of a lot of unmentionable things.

> 📖 When she finally cooled down, I said, rather quietly, "But this is how I am reading you."

> 📖 Of course, she saw what I was getting at immediately, and sputtered out like a spent candle. She simply did not know what to say. My example was artificial, of course, since I only pretended to read her in a certain way, but what I did was sufficient to prove

the point I was trying to make to her. "You are a deconstructionist," I told her, "but you expect me to interpret your words aright. More precisely, you are upset because I seem to be divorcing the meaning I claim to see in your words from your intent. Thus, implicitly you affirm the link between text and authorial intent. I have never read a deconstructionist who would be pleased if a reviewer misinterpreted his or her work: thus *in practice* deconstructionists implicitly link their own texts with their own intentions. I simply want the same courtesy extended to Paul."[36]

Carson concludes by saying that most people expect us to say what we mean and mean what we say. Although communication is often difficult and takes time, it is usually possible. If we hope to communicate the gospel message accurately, we better thoughtfully invest time in preparing ourselves for the task.

If you lack confidence in your faith, read 1 John, and highlight every place John tells us that we can know or how we can know something.

So is anything right about postmodernism?

The preceding description of postmodernism is a general summary. While all postmodernists may not embrace every aspect of the description above, it is a helpful synopsis.

Dennis McCallum cites five things he sees as correct in postmodern thought:

1. Without the infinite-personal creator God of the Bible, knowledge and reason do indeed become uncertain.
2. People are more subjective than they like to admit.
3. Our culture can, and often does, blind our eyes to truth obvious to other cultures and which, in retrospect, may also be clear to us.
4. People are social beings, and our social or cultural setting shapes and informs our values and thinking.
5. Blind faith in our legal status quo is unwarranted.[37]

---

[36] Carson, *The Gagging of God.* pp.102-103. Earl Radmacher tells of a similar experience in "A Response to Author's Intention and Biblical Interpretation." *Hermeneutics, Inerrancy, and the Bible,* edited by Radmacher and Preus, Academie Books, 1984, pp.433-444.

[37] McCallum, *Death of Truth.* pp.241-244.

Some have further argued that postmodernism has also helped many people realize that our confidence in the natural sciences to solve our problems and answer our questions is unjustifiable.

While we must be aware of these characteristics of postmodern thought that McCallum lists above, we must not simply embrace them as our own. For example, number one above suggests that postmodernists conclude knowledge and reason are uncertain because they do not know the God of the Bible. But even a godless postmodernist is sure of some knowledge.

The second statement in his list may be factual, but it fails to point us to the objective truth of the Bible. And while number four is also a fact, Christians must have our values and thinking transformed by a biblical worldview, because as children of our culture, our values and thinking have been deformed by our world.

We should be careful not to view postmodernists in terms of black and white. Whatever is useful about their philosophical position should be used to accomplish Kingdom goals. For example, postmodernists emphasize personal experience, and we invite them to experience the same rebirth that we experienced.

Postmodernism and the Church

Postmodernism is negatively affecting our churches. If you doubt this, listen to discussions about ethics and morality, and you will hear relativism and pragmatism. Listen to discussions about the meaning of a particular Bible text, and you will hear logic discarded in favor of subjective feelings ("What does this Bible text mean to you?"). Listen to the music in many churches and you will hear substance abandoned and style exalted. Do the people who attend your church treat the place of corporate worship as a sanctuary (and holy) or as an auditorium (just a place to listen to someone speak)?

Many of the ills that affect our churches today can be traced to the current cultural shift to postmodernism. Several books listed in the bibliography can help you document this.

If we restructure our church services to reach postmodernist non-Christians and to minister to postmodern Christians, who will minister to these (older?) members whose needs are not met in a service aimed at postmodernists? Church leaders must not ignore this question.

> ✎ Record in your journal some examples of the influence of postmodernism that you have seen in church life. Don't merely criticize a church or pastor, but list examples without naming people. How can we minimize this influence of postmodernism in the church? Is the Gospel supposed to be non-confrontational? Writing your thoughts in your journal helps you to develop them.

Two crucial needs are common among Christians today: (1) We need to develop our critical thinking abilities, and (2) We need to exercise the spiritual gift of discernment. Frankly, we Christians often do not know what is going on in the world around us, so we cannot use this knowledge for the Kingdom.

✝ *The Pharisees and Sadducees came to Jesus and tested him by asking him to show them a sign from heaven. He replied, "When evening comes, you say, 'It will be fair weather, for the sky is red,' and in the morning, 'Today it will be stormy, for the sky is red and overcast.' You know how to interpret the appearance of the sky, but you cannot interpret the signs of the times." (Matthew 16:1-3)*

Many Christians today also fail to understand the times in which we live. But if we are going to fulfill our calling as Christ's ambassadors, we will have to understand both God's Word and the people of our culture.

> ✎ If you are unsure what you could have gained from reading this chapter, read Rich Tatum's reaction in the Appendix: "Cognitive Reflections of a Dissonant Gen-Xer" (page 145). Record your reactions in your journal. Are your reactions similar or different?

Christianity is not just a blind leap of faith. We have the testimony of those who were present and pass on their empirical evidence.

✒ *That which was from the beginning, which we have heard, which we have seen with our eyes, which we have looked at and our hands have touched—this we proclaim concerning the Word of life. (1 John 1:1)*

An obstacle to witnessing

The postmodern worldview has made it difficult to witness to many of the people in our culture. As you have seen, postmodernists typically embrace the position that all truth is relative. Since there are no absolute truths, they usually do not accept the authority of the Scriptures. Since they have concluded there is no metanarrative, they usually conclude there is no Metanarrator too. For these reasons, the only revelation of God and the Gospel your postmodern friends may ever see is *your life*.

Jesus Christ...the faithful witness
Revelation 1:5

Chapter 3
Is Witnessing Optional?

God's commands vs. our traditions

In Mark 7, Jesus scolded the Jews for abusing one of their traditions. By declaring property *Corban*, a Jew dedicated it to the Temple and God's use—although the gift-giver retained control of the property. This meant it could not be used for anything else—including the support of aged parents. Jesus chastised them with these few sentences:

✟ *"You have a fine way of setting aside the commands of God in order to observe your own traditions!" (v.9)*

✟ *"Thus you nullify the word of God by your tradition that you have handed down. And you do many things like that." (v.13)*

Have we also ignored God's word in order to live out our own church traditions?

> ✎ Read Matthew 6 and see if you find any common traditions that we follow by ignoring the Scriptures. (Specifically consider each of these as a unit: verses 1-4, 5-8, and 19-21.) Is this ignoring the Bible to practice our traditions applicable to our witnessing habits?

Are Christians today in a similar situation in our witnessing? I hope you will keep this question in mind as you continue reading. If one day you conclude that you have fallen into this trap, I pray you will allow God to change your faith-walk.

Distinguishing characteristics of Christians

What distinguishes Christians from non-Christians? Most of us would probably identify love as the distinguishing characteristic of a believer. Jesus said:

✝ *"By this all men will know that you are my disciples, if you love one another." (John 13:35)*

Another distinguishing characteristic of a person who has experienced God's forgiveness is that he or she wants to tell others what has happened so that they can have the same experience.

During part of his earthly ministry, Jesus instructed some people to tell no one who he was or what he had done. Here are a couple of examples. Notice the result in the second example.

🕊 *Then he warned his disciples not to tell anyone that he was the Christ. (Matthew 16:20)*

🕊 *Jesus commanded them not to tell anyone [what he had done]. But the more he did so, the more they kept talking about it. (Mark 7:36)*

How the tables are turned today. We have been commanded to tell everyone, but today we remain silent! Consider the response of Peter and John when the Sanhedrin warned them to stop speaking about Jesus:

🕊 *"We cannot help speaking about what we have seen and heard." (Acts 4:20)*

Witnessing won't make you a Christian, but being a Christian will make you a witness. Dear God, let us have this attitude of Peter and John!

Why witness?

Why should you witness? The most obvious answer is that your Lord has commanded you to tell people what the Savior has done for you. But Westerners typically recoil at the idea of being told what to do—we value our freedom too much. God help us!

Our love for God and for people—the distinguishing marks of a Christian—should be a driving force behind our witnessing. Paul told the Christians in Corinth that

🕊 *Christ's love compels us, because we are convinced that one died for all, and therefore all died. And he died for all, that those who live should no longer live for themselves but for him who died for them and was raised again. (2 Corinthians 5:14-15)*

If we have been born again, God's Spirit lives in us, producing the fruit of the Spirit—including love. Christians witness because this is part of the new character the Spirit produces in us.

The typical response of one who has had a great debt cancelled is overwhelming joy and a desire to tell someone of that joy. (Read Luke 7:36-50.) So our joy at being forgiven makes us want to tell others.

Is your love for Christ and people the motivating force behind your attempts to witness—or is it something else? If it is guilt, you need to acquire a different motivation. Guilt is typically a poor motivator—and unbiblical. To act on guilt in order to appease God is to deny that Christ's atonement for our sin is sufficient. In other words, you are indicating that your works (in this case, witnessing) are necessary for your saving relationship with Christ. Contrast these two motivators: guilt is feelings-oriented; character is an inner reality. We must learn to distinguish between the guilt that Satan would inflict on us, and the sorrow that God's Holy Spirit may use to transform our character. Paul wrote:

Godly sorrow brings repentance that leads to salvation and leaves no regret. (2 Corinthians 7:10)

On the other hand, Satan is described as the accuser of the brethren (Revelation 12:10). Let God motivate you to witness and refuse to accept any feelings of guilt the devil would try to put in your mind.

God's Spirit can change your motivation from guilt to obedience borne out of love. As you read and reflect on these passages, ask God's Spirit to change your heart.

✝ *"Whoever acknowledges me before men, I will also acknowledge him before my Father in heaven. But whoever disowns me before men, I will disown him before my Father in heaven." (Matthew 10:32-33)*

✝ *Then Jesus came to them and said, "All authority in heaven and on earth has been given to me. Therefore go and make disciples of all nations, baptizing them in the name of the Father and of the Son and of the Holy Spirit, and teaching them to obey everything I have commanded you. And surely I am with you always, to the very end of the age." (Matthew 28:18-20)*

✝ *"But you will receive power when the Holy Spirit comes on you; and you will be my witnesses in Jerusalem, and in all Judea and Samaria, and to the ends of the earth." (Acts 1:8)*

All this is from God, who reconciled us to himself through Christ and gave us the ministry of reconciliation: that God was reconciling the world to himself in Christ, not counting men's sins against them. And he has committed to us the message of reconciliation. We are therefore Christ's ambassadors, as though God were making his appeal through us. We implore you on Christ's behalf: Be reconciled to God. (2 Corinthians 5:18-20)

✎ How do these Scripture passages affect your thinking about witnessing? What other Scriptures have shaped your thoughts on witnessing?

I ask you again: In regard to witnessing, have we set aside the clear commands of God in order to follow human traditions?

A biblical worldview inspires us to witness

Allowing the Bible to shape your worldview will motivate Christians to witness. Specifically, a biblical worldview will mold your concept of human history, Christ's return, physical death, and the final judgment.

Many people view history as evolutionary, that is, humans are constantly developing into better people. Others view history as cyclical, claiming that we are doomed to repeat the errors of the past. But the Bible presents human history as eschatological and teleological, that is moving toward a goal and purpose—and that goal is the return of Christ Jesus and the Judgment Day to fulfill God's purposes. Almost 2000 years ago the writers of Holy Scripture described the return of Christ as "soon." (Rev.22:20) If it was soon then, how much nearer it is today?

Closely connected to this imminent return of Christ is judgment. Both Old and New Testaments warn us of a coming Day of Judgment. The fact that this is an unpopular thought to many Westerners should not prevent us from confidently believing it, teaching it, and letting this fact inform our witness to the world.

Young people typically do not consider their own mortality. Perhaps the fact that so many live in an urban setting in which they do not see the death of the animals they eat contributes to this. Added to this is the fact that people die in a hospital more often than people die at home surrounded by family. All of this is just to say that people often do not see death but are somewhat shielded from it. The writer of Hebrews reminded his readers that "man is destined to die once, and after that to face judgment." (Hebrews 9:27)

Before you can witness

Being able to witness to God's saving power has a prerequisite. In a court of law, you can testify only to what you have seen. Similarly, you can legitimately witness only to what you have experienced. Jesus told Nicodemus, "You must be born again." (John 3:3) That is the absolute precondition for witnessing to the person and work of Christ Jesus.

Many church members are second-generation Christians—I call them "Church Kids." Some Church Kids have never personally experienced the rebirth Jesus spoke of. They grew up in the church, their parents were probably genuine Christians, but they only know about Jesus. So we should follow Paul's admonition to the Christians in Corinth:

☞ *Examine yourselves to see whether you are in the faith; test yourselves. Do you not realize that Christ Jesus is in you—unless, of course, you fail the test? And I trust that you will discover that we have not failed the test. (2 Corinthians 13:5-6)*

Church Kids typically go down one of three roads: the Road of Rebellion, the Road of Role Playing, or the Road of Reality. Those who follow the Road of Rebellion reject the Gospel, often so they can be their own masters. Others travel the Road of Role playing—they continue going to church and playing the part of a Christian, but they have never been born again. Those who have found the Road of Reality have had a personal experience with God by accepting the person and work of Christ Jesus.

I know all three roads by experience. If you discover that you're on either of the first two roads, I pray that you will find the third. The first two end in death; the third, in everlasting life! Choose life.

Christians should periodically re-examine ourselves. Not just to certain that we have been born again, but to see that we are genuinely trying to grow in our faith-walk, to become more like Jesus, to mature in obedience.

This self-examination should be done within the context of the local church. The great Apostle Paul submitted his gospel message to the leaders in Jerusalem (Galatians 2), and we will be wise to do the same periodically. The local church provides the believer with a measure of safety by helping to establish right doctrine and right living. Don't discard the protection the Body gives you.

27

Why don't Christians witness?

Christians fail to witness for a variety of reasons. Some of these reasons reflect the influence of our postmodern culture in our lives. How many of the reasons listed below have applied to you at different times?

Fear of rejection. No one likes to try to dialogue with someone and be rebuffed or treated with scorn and contempt. Experiencing this type of rejection makes us more hesitant to witness the next time we have an opportunity.

Doctrinal ignorance. Suspicion that you will appear ignorant or that you will be inadequate to the task may be another reason we don't witness. Too many Christians do not know what they believe, and if they do, they often are not sure why they believe what they say they believe.

Fear of making mistakes. Some Christians do not witness because they fear they will make mistakes. Will you make mistakes? Almost certainly. But you must not let this stop you. Everyone who has been a witness has made mistakes. We learn from them, trust the Lord to cover them and correct them, and go on.

Fear of failure. Westerners typically prize success. We cannot tolerate failure or being perceived by others as having failed in some way. But *not witnessing* is a failure.

Doubt of humankind's lost condition. Perhaps some folks are not convinced that non-Christians are really lost—in spite of the profusion of Bible texts that emphasize humankind's universal need for God's forgiveness (e.g., Romans 2:12; 3:10-24). From start to finish the Bible declares humanity's universal need for God's salvation.

Cultural peer pressure. Another reason we Christians fail to witness is that we are children of our postmodern, relativistic, pluralistic, hyper-tolerant culture. As such, many of us know that witnessing is not currently politically correct. Regrettably, many Christians are much more affected by peer pressure than we are by the commands of our Lord. As Eyre claimed, the characteristics of our culture have infiltrated and deformed the minds of Christians too.[38]

---

[38] See chapter 1 and the Appendix.

The exclusivity of the Gospel. This claim to exclusivity is the scandal of New Testament Christianity—and especially so in this postmodern age! Do you believe the Bible is trustworthy and accurately communicates what Jesus said and taught? Do you believe what Jesus said is true? If you do, you can reach only one conclusion because Jesus said,

✝ *"I am the way and the truth and the life. No one comes to the Father except through me." (John 14:6)*

This exclusivity may not be politically correct, but it is the plain teaching of the New Testament.

A lack of love. The reluctant evangelist-prophet Jonah did not want to travel to Nineveh and proclaim God's message to those people for a very simple reason—he hated them. And with some good reason, for these Assyrian soldiers were cruel to Israel. Listen to Jonah complain to God for sparing the Ninevites:

✝ *But Jonah was greatly displeased and became angry. He prayed to the LORD, "O LORD, is this not what I said when I was still at home? That is why I was so quick to flee to Tarshish. I knew that you are a gracious and compassionate God, slow to anger and abounding in love, a God who relents from sending calamity." (Jonah 4:1-2)*

But God responded to Jonah's anger over the loss of his shade-vine with this comment:

✝ *But the LORD said, "You have been concerned about this vine, though you did not tend it or make it grow. It sprang up overnight and died overnight. But Nineveh has more than a hundred and twenty thousand people who cannot tell their right hand from their left, and many cattle as well. Should I not be concerned about that great city?" (Jonah 4:10-11)*

May God help us to love non-Christians the way God loves non-Christians. We can say that we love the lost all we want to, but if we refuse to tell them the Gospel, we fail to do love to them. We are unable to produce this love ourselves, but—according to Galatians 5:22—the Holy Spirit will create this in us.

A lack of faith in the power of God. I wonder if we fail to witness at times because a particular person seems so bad and evil that we doubt God could save him or her. Don't discount God's power. Do you really believe God can save the vilest sinner? I once visited a man in a state penitentiary who was serving life for murder—he had bombed a house of worship. He was a white

29

supremacist who hated African-Americans and Jews. Shortly after arriving at the penitentiary, he came to faith in Christ, and God gave him a love for all people—including his African-American cellmate. Satan may be powerful, but God is all-powerful!

Cultural Christianity. In 1994, Barna described the influence of our culture and the decline of the Church like this:

> 📖 Three years ago, one of the danger signs was that most born-again Christians (52%) sided with the national majority in accepting relative truth as the standard. Sadly, an above average acceptance of relativism among believers has occurred in the intervening year. Currently, 62% of all born-again adults say there is no such thing as absolute truth. Amazingly, close to half of all evangelical Christians (42%) also reject absolutes when it comes to truth.[39]

This certainly helps to explain the situation the Church finds herself in today! Our churches have too many members who may be *christian* in a cultural sense, but they are not genuinely *Christians* in the biblical sense. Many of us have ignored Paul's admonition:

> ✍ *Do not conform any longer to the pattern of this world, but be transformed by the renewing of your mind. Then you will be able to test and approve what God's will is—his good, pleasing and perfect will. (Romans 12:2)*

Having our minds transformed by God's Word and God's Spirit takes time and is often hard work. We must recognize that we Christians are also children of our culture in need of having our minds renewed and transformed by the Holy Spirit.

> ✎ Make notes in your journal citing your own struggles and successes with witnessing. Be candid. The notes are for you and no one else.

The tyranny of time. Do you know anyone who does not complain of being too busy? Most of my Christian friends and colleagues frequently complain of being too busy. Yet all of us have the same 24 hours in a day and seven days in a week. If we do not have the time to build relationships with lost people, if we do not have the time to share a significant witness, then we need to re-prioritize our lives.

---

[39] George Barna, *Virtual America*. Regal Books, 1994, pp.83-84.

The missing essential ingredient. I've said it before, and I'll say it again: Some people do not—cannot—witness because they have never had a personal rebirth experience. If you have never been able to witness, you would do well to reflect on the reality of your own salvation. Consider Paul's exhortation one more time:

🕊 *Examine yourselves to see whether you are in the faith; test yourselves. Do you not realize that Christ Jesus is in you—unless, of course, you fail the test? (2 Corinthians 13:5)*

This list of reasons is not intended to be complete. Often these factors synergistically produce apathetic church members who have no passion for the lost.

Read back over this list of reasons Christians do not witness and identify and highlight the ones that describe you. Identifying the problem is just the first step in solving it. Now you'll have to allow God's Spirit to do in your life what Jesus said he would do:

✟ *"But you will receive power when the Holy Spirit comes on you; and you will be my witnesses..." (Acts 1:8)*

Whatever our reasons for not witnessing, they are woefully inadequate because they are unacceptable to God. By the power of the Holy Spirit, God's great grace, *and disciplined learning,* we can do what he has commissioned us to do. And one day we will hear him say to us,

✟ *"Well done, good and faithful servant! You have been faithful with a few things; I will put you in charge of many things. Come and share your master's happiness!" (Matthew 25:21)*

After being taken before the Sanhedrin, Peter and John returned to a group of Christians and reported that they had been commanded to stop preaching the Gospel or else they would face punishment. How did these Christians respond to threats? Did they pray for God to stop this persecution? Here's Luke's account:

🕊 *Now, Lord, consider their threats and enable your servants to speak your word with great boldness. (Acts 4:29)*

How did God answer their prayers?

🕊 *After they prayed, the place where they were meeting was shaken. And they were all filled with the Holy Spirit and spoke the word of God boldly. (Acts 4:31)*

31

🖉 Once I attempted to write a letter to a postmodern friend. Turn to page 149 in the Appendix, find and read this letter. In light of what you have learned in these first two chapters, critique my letter. What should have been worded differently? What was said that shouldn't have been said? What was omitted that should have been included? Try to write your own letter in your journal along with your critique of my attempt.

We are...Christ's ambassadors
2 Corinthians 5:20

Chapter 4
What Do You Want Me to Say, God?

What is a witness?

Perhaps one reason some Christians do not witness is that they are unsure what it is that they must say to the lost. Are there certain parts of the Bible you should quote? Must they be quoted in a certain order? What if you cannot answer someone's question—or answer it to his or her satisfaction? Peter exhorts his readers to prepare themselves for this very occasion.

> *But in your hearts set apart Christ as Lord. Always be prepared to give an answer to everyone who asks you to give the reason for the hope that you have. But do this with gentleness and respect, keeping a clear conscience...(1 Peter 3:15-16)*

Notice that one element of a biblical witness is answering the questions of the lost person. Also, the foundation of our preparation for answering these questions is the rule (lordship) of Christ in our hearts.

In other words, Peter tells us that we Christians should be ready to tell someone what we have experienced. In a nutshell it is this:

1. God helped us to see ourselves as sinners who would ultimately receive punishment for our sins. (Romans 3:23)
2. God used someone to communicate his love and offer of forgiveness through Jesus' payment for our sins. (Romans 5:8)
3. God gave us the faith to turn away from sin and ask him for forgiveness by believing him and completely placing our faith in him to save us. (Romans 10:8-13)
4. God's Holy Spirit convinced us of our forgiveness, changed us, entered us, and became our Ruler. (Romans 5:5; 15:13, 16)
5. Since becoming our Ruler, God has been continuing to change our desires and thinking—although none of us has reached perfection. (Romans 12:1-3)

Closely connected to this fear that we don't know what to say to the lost is the added apprehension that we do not understand the entire

33

gospel message well enough to witness. But you don't have to know everything in order to be a credible witness. Sure, the more you know, the better you may be able to witness to someone. But the Gospel has only a few "essential elements," and you probably already know most of them and can certainly learn the rest. Paul provides a useful summary of them in 1 Corinthians 15:3-8:

🕊 *For what I received I passed on to you as of first importance: that Christ died for our sins according to the Scriptures, that he was buried, that he was raised on the third day according to the Scriptures, and that he appeared to Peter, and then to the Twelve. After that, he appeared to more than five hundred of the brothers at the same time, most of whom are still living, though some have fallen asleep. Then he appeared to James, then to all the apostles, and last of all he appeared to me.*

Of course, these few sentences assume several other things. For example, saying "Christ died for our sins" says something about our being sinners and our fate as sinners. Saying "according to the Scriptures" says something about the authority of the Scriptures.

But my point is simply this: the core of the Gospel has to do with:
1. Who Jesus Christ is and what he did.
2. Who humans are, our purpose in life, and what we need.

Any person who has experienced God's salvation can communicate these to a friend with very little practice.

One of my colleagues includes four essentials in a gospel witness:
1. God presented as holy, just, and loving.
2. Humankind's condition apart from God's grace.
3. Jesus as the only way to the Father, who he is, and what he did on the cross of Calvary.
4. Humankind's proper response: repentance and faith that results in obedience.[40]

With very little practice every Christian can explain these to anyone who will listen.

---

[40] Personal communication from Rev. Thomas Keinath, Central Bible College.

What a witness is not

We might better understand what a witness *is* by considering what it *is not*. It is not a sermon. People who cannot preach, can still witness. Further, witnessing does not necessarily involve striking up a conversation with total strangers and talking with them about their eternal salvation—though some Christians will do this. I thank God for the people who are so gifted that they can quickly and easily talk with a stranger about spiritual matters without alienating them. But not every Christian has this gift; so don't feel guilty if you don't. Instead, use the gifts God has given you.

Finally, some folks think just living the Christian life so that others can see it is an adequate witness. This story illustrates that concept.

> 📖 Cecil Northcott in *A Modern Epiphany* tells of a discussion in a camp of young people where representatives of many nations were living together. "One wet night the campers were discussing various ways of telling people about Christ. They turned to the girl from Africa. 'Maria,' they asked, 'what do you do in your country?' 'Oh,' said Maria, 'we don't have missions or give pamphlets away. We just send one or two Christian families to live and work in a village, and when people see what Christians are like, then they want to be Christians too.'" In the end, the only all-conquering argument is the argument of a life lived for Christ Jesus.[41]

Do Peter's words seem to support this?

> ✍ *Live such good lives among the pagans that, though they accuse you of doing wrong, they may see your good deeds and glorify God on the day he visits us. (1 Peter 2:12)*

Is just living a Christian life without telling others of the Lord enough? If you think it is, go back to Chapter 2 and read the words of Jesus again. A witness is not just the way you live your life, and it is not just words. But when your words match your life, that's a biblical witness that will draw even postmodernists!

What is the Gospel?

So many doctrines are connected with the Gospel that many Christians get confused about the relative merits of different

---

[41] Topic: Witnessing, Index: 3603-3605 in *Bible Illustrator* version 1.5d (computer software), Parsons Technology, Inc., 1990-1992.

doctrines. Do all doctrines have equal weight? Or are some doctrines more important than others? Have you ever considered this question?

> 🖉 Here is another valuable exercise to write in your journal. Construct three columns labeled "essential," "important," and "peripheral." Under "essential" list only those doctrines that you think a person must believe in order to be saved. Under "important" list those doctrines that you see as so important that if they do not know these truths their faith will quickly be jeopardized. Then under "peripheral" list those doctrines that are true, but variation here will not likely affect their faith walk to much extent. Got it? If you have trouble thinking of doctrines to list, look in the Appendix (page 158) for several doctrines listed in a random order and try to group them under these three headings. But make your own list first.

If you really want to think, do this with a friend and compare notes. All of the doctrines you list should be ones that you consider to be true because the Bible plainly teaches them.

Knowing what the Gospel is, what it is not, and the relative value of a variety of Bible doctrines provide a foundation on which to build a faith-walk that will allow you to witness confidently.

A central feature of the Gospel is that fact that we do not—cannot—earn God's forgiveness, but that he offers it to us as a free gift (pardon my redundancy). No one deserves God's forgiveness; we all deserve his punishment. Years ago a friend told me that God's mercy means that *he does not give me what I deserve*—death now; and that God's grace means that *he does give me what I don't deserve*—his forgiveness and eternal life!

The word *Gospel* comes from a word that means *good news*. If there is good news, what is the bad news? The Bible plainly teaches that God will one day judge and punish sinners. The fate of the ungodly is an unpopular aspect of the Gospel today, but it is an intrinsic part of the Gospel and must be part of a biblical witness. Jesus died to save sinners from hell, eternal separation from God. This should help motivate us to witness to the lost, and it should fill us with joy for our salvation. Don't be mislead: God's judgment is sure.

Carson argues—I think correctly—that the Gospel must be presented and should be received within the structure of a biblical worldview. He wrote:

36

📖 What I am arguing is that without this kind of structure the Gospel will not be rightly heard. The doctrine of Creation establishes the grounds of our responsibility before God: he made us for himself, and it is the essence of our culpable anarchy that we ignore it. The doctrine of the Fall establishes the nature of our dilemma: by nature and choice we are alienated from God, deceived, justly condemned, without hope in the world, unless God himself delivers us. All of our ills trail from this profound rebellion. Solutions that do not address our alienation from the personal/transcendent God who made us are at best superficial palliatives, at worst deceptive placebos that leave us to die.[42]

If he is correct, we have a huge task ahead of us just in order to establish an understanding of a biblical worldview in the minds of most postmodern Westerners.

Presentation matters

In a section titled "Who Needs a Parachute?" Ray Comfort suggests that the way the Gospel is presented makes a great deal of difference in the way a non-Christian responds. He used this illustration to make his point.

📖 Two men are seated in a plane. A stewardess gives the first man a parachute and instructs him to put it on because it will "improve his flight."

📖 Not understanding how a parachute could possibly improve his flight, the first passenger is a little skeptical. Finally he decides to see if the claim is true. After strapping on the parachute, he notices its burdensome weight, and he has difficulty sitting upright. Consoling himself with the promise of a better flight, our first passenger decides to give it a little time.

📖 Because he's the only one wearing a parachute, some of the other passengers begin smirking at him, which only adds to his humiliation. Unable to stand it any longer, our friend slumps in his seat, unstraps the parachute, and throws it to the floor. Disillusionment and bitterness fill his heart because as far as he is concerned, he was told a lie.

📖 Another stewardess gives the second man a parachute, *but listen to her instructions*. She tells him to put it on because at any moment he will be jumping out of the plane at 25,000 feet.

---

[42] Carson, *The Gagging of God.* p.504.

> 📖 Our second passenger gratefully straps the parachute on. He doesn't notice its weight upon his shoulders nor that he can't sit upright. His mind is consumed with the thought of what would happen to him if he jumped without it. When other passengers laugh at him, he thinks, "You won't be laughing when you're falling to the ground!"[43]

We need to present the Savior not merely as someone who will improve your life, but as your only hope of salvation from God's judgment for your sins! And this gospel is not socially acceptable or politically correct today.

"Who do you say I am?"

In the ninth chapter of Luke's Gospel, Jesus asks his disciples, "Who do the crowds say I am?" The disciples said that people were offering a variety of answers including John the Baptist, the Prophet Elijah, and one of the other Old Testament prophets. Then Jesus asked them, "Who do you say I am?" Peter replied, "The Christ of God" (Luke 9:20).

The single most important thing we have to tell people is who Jesus is. He alone must be the focus of our witness. The Old Testament sets the stage for our understanding the life and teachings of the Messiah. The Gospels provide four different perspectives on the Savior. The Book of Acts shows how the resurrected Lord continued the ministry he started when he walked the earth. The Epistles affirm the validity of the Gospels and Acts and teach us how to live out our faith in Jesus Christ. And Revelation tells us how it will all end with the return of Jesus as King of kings and Lord of lords.

Our testimony must be about him, not about us.

C. S. Lewis (Professor of Medieval and Renaissance English Literature, Cambridge University, England) said it so profoundly in his book *Mere Christianity* that it has been quoted repeatedly and is worthy of repetition here.

> 📖 I am trying here to prevent anyone saying the really foolish thing that people often say about Him: "I'm ready to accept Jesus as a great moral teacher, but I don't accept his claim to be God." That is the one thing we must not say. A man who was merely a man

---

[43] Ray Comfort, *Hell's Best Kept Secret*. Whitaker House, 1989, pp.10-11.

and said the sort of things Jesus said would not be a great moral teacher. He would either be a lunatic—on a level with the man who says he is a poached egg—or else he would be the Devil of Hell. You must take your choice. Either this man was, and is, the Son of God; or else a madman or something worse. You can shut him up for a fool, you can spit at Him and kill Him as a demon; or you can fall at His feet and call Him Lord and God. But let us not come with any patronizing nonsense about his being a great human teacher. He has not left that open to us. He did not intend to.[44]

Who are you telling people Jesus is? What does your life communicate to others about Jesus?

What does it mean to "believe in Jesus"?

In Acts, Luke tells us of Paul and Silas in jail in Philippi (because they had cast a demon out of a slave girl). About midnight an earthquake opened the doors of the jail and chains fell off the prisoners. When the jailer saw what had happened, he assumed his life was forfeit, so he started to end his own life. When Paul prevented this drastic action, the jailer asked Paul, "What must I do to be saved?" Paul answered, "Believe in the Lord Jesus, and you will be saved..." (Acts 16:30-31). This echoed the words of Jesus in John 3:16, 18.

> ✎ Imagine you are witnessing to an unbelieving friend. How would you explain the phrase "believe in the Lord Jesus" to this friend?

If you are going to witness to people, you had better be prepared not only to tell them to believe in the Lord Jesus, you had also better be prepared to explain what this means. Believing in Jesus does not merely mean believing certain things about Jesus are true. It does not mean merely believing that the doctrines of Christianity are true. James told his readers,

> *You believe that there is one God. Good! Even the demons believe that—and shudder. (James 2:19)*

Believing in Jesus goes beyond this intellectual or mental assent.
Paul summed it up well in his letter to the Romans.

---

[44] C. S. Lewis, "The Shocking Alternative" in *Mere Christianity*. Macmillan Publishing Co., 1957. pp.40-41.

> ✍ *If you confess with your mouth, "Jesus is Lord," and believe in your heart that God raised him from the dead, you will be saved. For it is with your heart that you believe and are justified, and it is with your mouth that you confess and are saved. (Romans 10:9-10)*

Believing in Jesus means letting him rule your life. This involves a commitment to obedience that goes far beyond embracing a proposition. This is a not just an alignment with a creed but a commitment to God's Son.

What is left if you take Christ out of Christianity? Just *ianity*—and that doesn't mean anything. Christianity without Christ is totally meaningless.

Your assignment

Your assignment is to love people—not only the beautiful, popular, loveable, godly, slim, clean, and smart people, but also the ugly, fat, ignorant, unpopular, unlovely, ungodly, dirty, and dumb people. Be a friend to sinners as Jesus was.

Characteristics of an effective witness

A biblical witness will:
- Exalt Jesus as Messiah and Lord
- Be motivated by love
- Respect the hearer
- Be controlled by and use biblical truth
- Be presented boldly yet humbly
- Be empowered by the Holy Spirit
- Typically tell others what God has done and is doing in your life
- Be authenticated by a lifestyle consistent with all of the above

---

✐ Choose one of the exercises in the Exercises to Develop Strategy in the Appendix (pages 174-175). Begin trying to construct a witnessing strategy to this fictional person. You'll work more on this later.

---

*Not that we are competent in ourselves to claim anything
for ourselves, but our competence comes from God*
2 Corinthians 3:5

Chapter 5
Put These in Your Tackle Box

The role of the Bible

What you believe about the Bible today will in large part determine where your faith will be five or ten years from now. Some see it as a "good book." Others think it "contains God's Word," leaving them to choose which parts of the Bible are not God's Word. If you will accept it as our only authority in matters of faith and practice, you will be spared many griefs.

Without question the Bible should play a controlling part in our witness. If our experiences with the Lord—both in salvation and in SANCTIFICATION—are the subjective element of the Christian life, then the Scriptures are the objective part.

Those who claim the Bible as the sole authority in matters of faith and practice should allow the Bible to control the content of our witnessing. What claims do the Scriptures make about themselves?[45] First, the Bible is God's Word, and that makes it authoritative.

🕊 *Above all, you must understand that no prophecy of Scripture came about by the prophet's own interpretation. For prophecy never had its origin in the will of man, but men spoke from God as they were carried along by the Holy Spirit. (2 Peter 1:20-21)*

🕊 *But as for you, continue in what you have learned and have become convinced of, because you know those from whom you learned it, and how from infancy you have known the holy Scriptures, which are able to make you wise for salvation through faith in Christ Jesus. All Scripture is God-breathed and is useful for teaching, rebuking, correcting and training in righteousness, so that the man of God may be thoroughly equipped for every good work. (2 Timothy 3:14-18)*

---

[45] Of course, we know that when the New Testament writers referred to the Scriptures, they were referring to the Old Testament. But Christians typically believe the principles described in these texts apply to the New Testament, too.

Many Christians think the New Testament alone is sufficient for witnessing to the lost and for teaching new converts. If you are in this group, you need to realize that the Old Testament provides us with the background to understand what "Jesus is Christ" means. In his earthly ministry, Jesus used the Old Testament in his teaching repeatedly. Further, the New Testament writings quote the Old Testament hundreds of times. Beyond that, in his letters, Paul used the Old Testament to argue for the Gospel. He gives us other clear indications of the value of the Old Testament history to the life of the believer:

⊱ *For everything that was written in the past was written to teach us, so that through endurance and the encouragement of the Scriptures we might have hope. (Romans 15:4)*

⊱ *Now these things occurred as examples to keep us from setting our hearts on evil things as they did. (1 Corinthians 10:6)*

We would be foolish to discard this valuable body of instruction.

✎ Years ago a Christian acquaintance criticized the words of the old gospel song: "You ask me how I know he lives, he lives within my heart." "No," he said, "the only way we know Jesus lives is the Bible tells us so." Do you agree? Explain and defend your answer in your journal.

The role of prayer

Prayer includes listening to God. If prayer is two-way communication with God, which do you think is more important—what you have to tell him, or what he has to tell you? Let your answer shape your prayer life. Do you see why prayer and Bible study go hand-in-hand?

Prayer constantly reminds us of our total dependence on God's power to accomplish his will and purpose in our lives. We need to ask God to give us the right motivation to witness, to direct us to the right people, to give us the right words, to convict the lost, to convince them of the truth of the Gospel, and, ultimately, to bring them to repentance and to convert them.

God may lead you to pray with non-Christians concerning their needs. Don't just do this on your own. Follow the leading of the Spirit. But God may use answered prayer to create faith in their hearts and minds.

Paul's exhortation to the believers in 1 Thessalonians 5:17—"Pray without ceasing"—is appropriate for Christians who would witness too.

> ✎ How does your prayer life need to develop in order for you to become a more consistent witness? Do you pray for boldness and wisdom? Do you pray for direction in choosing people to witness to? Do you pray for lost friends and relatives? Respond in your journal.

The old slogan "Prayer Changes Things" is a poor paraphrase of Scriptural teaching. (My apologies to those who hold this as their favorite Christian cliché.) If you immediately think of Romans 8:28, please consider the fact that most modern English translations do a much better job of translating this passage than the King James Version did.

> ℘ *And we know that all things work together for good to them that love God, to them who are the called according to his purpose. (Romans 8:28, King James Version)*

Think about it. Even a New Age adherent could agree with that. This just says, "things will work out." Other modern English translations say something like the *New International Version* does:

> ℘ *And we know that in all things God works for the good of those who love him, who have been called according to his purpose.*

See the difference? The focus is really on God, not on our prayers or us. God changes things—sometimes when we have not even prayed!

The role of the Holy Spirit

No one simply decides to trust and follow Jesus as Lord and Savior on his or her own. The third person of the Trinity works from the beginning, through conversion, and on through sanctification. Jesus told his disciples:

> ♰ *"No one can come to me unless the Father who sent me draws him." John 6:44*
> ♰ *"No one can come to me unless the Father has enabled him." John 6:65*

The Holy Spirit reveals God to a person in many different ways: through the Scriptures, through the testimonies of Christians, through

43

the lives of people, and, at times, directly (as he did with Saul/Paul). But the Holy Spirit is involved in another way too.

Luke's quotation of Jesus in Acts 1:8 emphasizes the role of the Holy Spirit in empowering Christians to witness. All the education, training, and experiences in the world are no substitute for the empowerment of the Holy Spirit in witnessing. Consider the fruit of the Holy Spirit listed in Galatians 5:22-23:

> ✍ *The fruit of the Spirit is love, joy, peace, patience, kindness, good-ness, faithfulness, gentleness and self-control.*

> ✎ Is it obvious that these qualities will attract people to you and to Jesus? Is it obvious that the fruit of the Holy Spirit in your life is in itself a witness? Try to list some personal experiences (whether you were the one receiving the witness or giving the witness).

Although 1 Corinthians 12–14 addresses manifestations of God's power in the context of the assembly of Christians, Acts records these manifestations in the context of evangelism in the streets. An analysis of the Book of Acts shows that usually when the Apostles took the gospel message to a new place, the Holy Spirit validated the gospel message with a demonstration of God's power. I believe we can depend on God to do no less today as we proclaim his truth!

But even though it is true that "all the education, training, and experiences in the world are no substitute for the empowerment of the Holy Spirit in witnessing," God can use all of these to make you a better witness—if you rely on him and not on your abilities.

> ✎ Make notes on the fruit of the Spirit evidenced in your life that helps you witness and which fruit of the Spirit that you need to develop to help you witness. Virtually every Christian will find areas in which he or she can grow.

The New Testament also talks about gifts (or manifestations) of the Holy Spirit being produced in the lives of Christians. One list is found in 1 Corinthians 12:7-10.

> ✍ *Now to each one the manifestation of the Spirit is given for the common good. To one there is given through the Spirit the message of wisdom, to another the message of knowledge by means of the same Spirit, to another faith by the same Spirit, to another gifts of healing by that one Spirit, to another miraculous powers, to another prophecy, to another distinguishing between*

spirits, to another speaking in different kinds of tongues, and to still another the interpretation of tongues.

Another list is found in Romans 12:6-8.

🕊 *We have different gifts, according to the grace given us. If a man's gift is prophesying, let him use it in proportion to his faith. If it is serving, let him serve; if it is teaching, let him teach; if it is encouraging, let him encourage; if it is contributing to the needs of others, let him give generously; if it is leadership, let him govern diligently; if it is showing mercy, let him do it cheerfully.*

Do these gifts function in witnessing, too? I think some of them do, at least sometimes. In Acts 3 and 4 we read how God healed a crippled beggar through Peter and John. Because of this miraculous healing (a gift of the Holy Spirit named in 1 Corinthians 12), Peter and John were able to witness to the man who was healed, to the people who saw it, and to the Jewish leaders. Others of these gifts can help equip Christians to be witnesses (for example, faith, encouraging, and teaching).

🖋 Should we conclude that God has discarded the gifts of the Holy Spirit for Christians today? Offer reasons for your answer from the Scriptures and from personal experience. Which is weightier? Why?

Do you know which gifts the Holy Spirit has given you? Don't confuse the gifts of the Spirit with your natural talents or learned abilities. These are not the same. Several books have been published that can help you discover your spiritual gifts.[46] If you are not sure which gifts the Holy Spirit has given you, you should ask him to help you find out. Your close Christian friends may help too.

We shouldn't insist that God's Spirit speak audibly to us, directing us to each person to whom we should witness. Instead of praying, "God, let me know if you want me to witness to this friend," we should pray, "Lord, if you don't want me to witness to someone,

---

[46] For example, Tim Blanchard's *A Practical Guide to Finding and Using Your Spiritual Gifts*, Tyndale House, 1983. Bruce Bugbee's *What You Do Best in the Body of Christ*, Zondervan Publishing, 1995; Kenneth C. Kinghorn's *Discovering Your Spiritual Gifts: A Personal Inventory Method*, Francis Asbury Press, 1981; and C. Peter Wagner's *Your Spiritual Gifts Can Help Your Church Grow*, Regal Books, 1994, "Wagner-Modified Houts Questionnaire," (pp.237-259). Materials like these can help Christians understand themselves and their place in the church.

please keep him out of my circle of friends." As we stay sensitive to every "gentle nudge" of the Holy Spirit regarding the timing and content of our witness, we'll find the right way to share our faith with our family, friends, school-mates, and co-workers.

The role of power events

Luke records how God used supernatural events to validate the gospel message. These power events included tongues and preaching (Acts 2), healings (Acts 3 & 5), visions (Acts 10 & 16), exorcisms (Acts 16), people raised from the dead (Acts 20), divine punishment (Acts 5 & 12), jail breaks (Acts 12 & 16), blindness (Acts 13), conversions (Acts 9), and boldness in witnessing (Acts 4 & 7). Does God still use super-natural events today?

During my last year of doctoral studies, a young man I'll call Ron came to me in my research laboratory asking me if it was true that my wife and I had been separated, and now we were back together again. I was a little surprised since I barely knew Ron. "Yes," I said, "that's true." Then he began asking me many personal questions. I knew this was neither the time nor the place to discuss these things, so I suggested that he come over to my house that evening so we could have the time to explore the things he wished to discuss. He agreed.

That evening we sat on the back steps at my house, and he awkwardly began trying to tell me what the problems were. But while he was talking, the Holy Spirit was speaking in my mind telling me things about him and his marriage. I not only shocked Ron, I shocked myself when I looked at him and said, "Ron, you are having an affair aren't you?" He paused, but said nothing. Then I continued. "You are having an affair with Carol. You and your wife have been having problems for a long time, haven't you?" He nodded, and I went on to describe their marriage problems—things about which I could humanly know nothing. We were both stunned.

Finally I told Ron that his marriage problems were due to a larger problem: he was not trusting Christ as his Savior and Lord. Then Ron told me, "I knew I had to come and talk to you. I used to trust and follow the Lord, but I have been away from him for a long time." You won't be surprised to learn that before Ron left that night, we knelt and prayed together, and he committed his life anew to the Savior. He went home and told his wife of his new faith in God, and their marriage was transformed.

> 🖎 Do you think that Christians should anticipate that the Holy Spirit will always manifest himself like this? Can the believer decide when God will work in supernatural ways like this? How has God used you? Are you willing for God to use you, or do you put limits on him?

The role of good works

About five centuries ago the church suffered a major schism largely over two questions: (1) What is the ultimate Church authority, and (2) What role do faith and works have in our salvation? The Reformers's answers to these two questions were: The Bible is our sole authority in matters of faith and practice, and we are saved by faith in Christ Jesus alone. A typical proof text (among many) is frequently cited from Ephesians to support the second answer:

🖎 *For it is by grace you have been saved, through faith—and this not from yourselves, it is the gift of God—not by works, so that no one can boast. (Ephesians 2:8-9)*

If you grew up in church, many of you probably learned that passage as a youngster. But I wonder how many of you also learned the very next sentence. I've asked many people this question through the years and found that few—too few—knew the next sentence. Do you know it? Before you read on, try to recall it. Don't peek now. Did you remember it? It is:

🖎 *For we are God's workmanship, created in Christ Jesus to do good works, which God prepared in advance for us to do. (Ephesians 2:10)*

The very next sentence reminds us of the role of good works in the life of the Christian. Why weren't we taught this verse, too? Often when the pendulum has swung too far one way, and we attempt to correct it, we end up bringing it too far back the other way. The Church had overemphasized good works, probably for centuries. Now the Church is under-emphasizing them.

So let's try to put good works in proper, biblical perspective. Good works will not—cannot—save you. Paul's letters spell that out without question.[47] But saved people will do good works. James's letter spells that truth out in equal detail. And those good works will bring glory to God and in themselves provide a potent witness. This is illustrated in Peter's admonition to wives:

> *Wives, in the same way be submissive to your husbands so that, if any of them do not believe the word, they may be won over without words by the behavior of their wives, when they see the purity and reverence of your lives. (1 Peter 3:1-2)*

Further, those good works will draw the lost to the Savior, and they are a witness, both to the changed life of the Christian and the love of God. Jesus taught his followers to

> *"Let your light shine before men, that they may see your good deeds and praise your Father in heaven." (Matthew 5:16)*

Our good works point past the genuine Christian to the Lord. Doing good works will tire us, so Paul reminded us:

> *Let us not become weary in doing good, for at the proper time we will reap a harvest if we do not give up. (Galatians 6:9)*

So you should be looking for ways that God has opened the door for you to do good works. Then, don't be surprised when doing these good works provides you with the opportunity to witness to what God has done in your life. Expect it. God is doing his part.

Which good works should Christians expect to become involved in? Jesus specifically mentioned five in his end-time parable of the sheep and the goats in Matthew 25:31-46. These good works are feeding the hungry, giving water to the thirsty, giving hospitality to strangers, clothing the naked, caring for the sick, and visiting those in prison.

But I do not think he meant this to be an exhaustive list. Rather this list can be thought of as representative of the kinds of things Christians should be trying to do: meeting the needs of others.

The Old Testament taught similar values for the Jews. The negative parts of the Ten Commandments (Exodus 20) had positive implications. For example, the negative "You shall not give false testimony against your neighbor" (v.16), implies the positive "Tell the truth." Further, several of the laws in chapters 21 through 23 of Exodus speak of social responsibility. The books of Amos and Micah

---

[47] If you did not know this, read Paul's letter to Galatians and Romans 3 and 4.

instructed God's people of the good works he expected of them. You could read Isaiah 58:6-7 and Micah 6:6-8 to verify this.

> ✐ Which good works has God already had you involved in? Have you missed some opportunities to do good works? Why did you miss these? What changes can you make to fulfill this aspect of the Christian life? What happens to the believer who does good works from a right motivation?

The role of fasting

Many Christians never practice fasting as a spiritual discipline. But fasting is just as biblical—just as New Testament—as prayer. Re-read the Gospels to see how often Jesus and his disciples fasted and to examine Jesus' teachings on fasting (e.g., Matthew 6:16-17).

On the other hand, Christians who fast often misunderstand what it is for. Fasting does not empower us to leverage God into giving us what we want. Nothing we do changes the fact that he is God Almighty, and we are his servants.

Instead, fasting helps us to focus on spiritual realities and the task at hand.

When I was in graduate school, a church and a friend paid my way to Chicago to speak to a church group and visit. The first night there, as I was going to sleep, I was overcome with this waste of God's money. I was ashamed to think that I would think myself so important that we could waste a few hundred dollars of God's money to fly me to Chicago for four or five days.

So I prayed, "God, I will do anything you want me to do to make this a profitable trip for your kingdom." Every time I prayed this way, the Holy Spirit led me to fast. Finally I committed to God that I would fast.

At mealtime every day I walked across campus and sat on a bench to be by myself and pray. But a young lady named Anita used that bench at lunch every day too. Little did I know that we had a divine appointment, and my fast and her lunch provided a daily dialogue about the claims of the Gospel. On my last day there, Anita prayed to receive the Savior. My fast did not make it happen, but it put me in a place that God could use me.

The role of love

As noted earlier, typically postmodernists cannot tolerate the intolerance of Christians. (I hope you noticed the irony of this statement.) But Daniel Taylor asks:

📖 Must Christians be tolerant? Not really—certainly not as our society defines the term. But we must be loving, and that is a far greater challenge, with far greater dangers and rewards. We must find better ways to demonstrate that we do, in fact, love the sinner while we hate the sin.[48]

What a challenge! You will do this only with the help of the Holy Spirit.

Chapter 2 began by identifying love as a distinguishing characteristic of genuine Christians. In reply to a question from an expert in the Jewish law asking him to name the greatest law,

✝ *Jesus replied: "'Love the Lord your God with all your heart and with all your soul and with all your mind.' This is the first and greatest commandment. And the second is like it: 'Love your neighbor as yourself.' All the Law and the Prophets hang on these two commandments." (Matthew 22:37-40)*

He summed up for us the two-part foundation of our life and witnessing: our love for God and our love for people. Dennis McCallum distinguishes New Testament *love* from postmodernism's *respect.*

📖 Interestingly, while there is nothing inherently wrong with respect, the Bible seldom calls on us to respect one another, especially not in the postmodern sense. God calls us to *love* one another. And love *can* confront others with their error. Love *does* call for change from *your* way to the *other* way—to God's way. Like the postmodern concept of respect, love involves positive regard. But unlike postmodern respect, love doesn't tiptoe around human pride. It does what is good and right for another, not what the other demands. Postmodern respect is positive regard *without* judgment. Christian love is positive regard *with* judgment, in a constructive sense.[49]

Calvin Miller offers another illustration of the kind of love that we Christians need in order to be motivated to witness.

---

[48] Taylor, "Are You Tolerant?" *Christianity Today.* January 11, 1999, p.52.
[49] McCallum, *The Death of Truth.* p.241.

📖 Love reaches for the hurt and takes bold steps without self-interest. It can accomplish unbelievable things merely because it is so void of self-interest.

📖 Some time ago, a teenager, Arthur Hinkley, lifted a 3,000-pound tractor with bare hands. He wasn't a weight lifter, but his friend, Lloyd Bachelder, 18, was pinned under a tractor on a farm near Rome, Maine. Hearing Lloyd scream, Arthur somehow lifted the tractor enough for Lloyd to wriggle out.

📖 Love was the real motivation.[50]

Do you know anyone that you love so much that you want to lift the weight of sin off his or her life? Or are you just too preoccupied with your own interests?

Often we think of doing love to people in our church to the exclusion of the unchurched. In their book *Death and the Caring Community*, Larry Richards and Paul Johnson repeat a story told by Ralph Neighbour (pastor of West Memorial Baptist Church, Houston, Texas). He told how a group of Christian men once responded in love to the need of a non-Christian.

📖 "It started when I was giving my deacons some training in terminal personality stages. One of my men said, 'Next time you visit someone going through this, I'd like to come.' So I took him with me to see Jack.

📖 "Jack had cancer in the lower part of his body. He'd already had a colostomy, and had almost no lower body functions. We visited with him in his bathrobe, in his home. His wife was also there. This was my second or third visit, and I was just trying to relate to them.

📖 "Jack had been president of a large corporation, and when he got cancer they ruthlessly dumped him. He had run through his insurance at this point, and used his life savings, and had practically nothing left.

📖 "I had told my deacon to listen, but not say anything. But in the middle of it my deacon just had to witness. He said, 'Jack, you speak so openly about the shortness of the life you have left. I'm sure you've thought very much about dying. I wonder if you've prepared for your life after your death?'

📖 "Jack stood up, livid with rage. He tottered there in his bathrobe, shaking and cursing. 'You—Christians,' he shouted. 'All you ever think about is what's going to happen to me after I die. I don't

---

[50] Calvin Miller, "Rethinking Suburban Evangelism," *Leadership*, Fall 1988, p.68.

know that anything will, and I don't care. If your God is so great, why doesn't He do something about the real problems of life?'

📖 "Enraged, Jack went on to tell us that he was leaving his wife penniless. He was leaving his daughter without a college education. He was going out with a whimper, not able to provide a thing for them. And with that he ordered us to get out.

📖 "We got outside and I said, 'You see what can happen. You went right past the man's feelings. You mirrored your own values across to him, and assumed that your values would be his, when in fact he has a totally different structure of concern.'"

This story did little to inspire me—in fact, I was quite disappointed. But to my relief, later in their book, Richards and Johnson continued quoting Pastor Neighbour.

📖 "Later my deacon insisted I take him back, which I did not want to do. He said, 'I'm either going with or without you, and I think we'd both feel better if you went with me.' So we went. The wife refused to let us in. I begged her. I said, 'I know we made him angry before. But this is very, very important.'

📖 "Finally she let us go in. He was in bed. He'd gotten considerably weaker over the last week.

📖 "This deacon pulled out a little note pad and said, 'Jack, I know I offended you before. I humbly apologize. But I want you to know I've been working since then.

📖 "'Your first problem is how will your wife and daughter have a place to live when she doesn't have any income. I checked in the neighborhood. You've owned this house for X number of years; I compute you have a minimum of X dollars in the house. We have a realtor in the church who's agreed to sell your house, and give your widow the real estate commission.

📖 "'I guarantee you that a group of men along with me will make the payments for any months that might elapse till the house is sold. So stay here till you die, and if you'll permit me, we'll make your payments.

📖 "'Then, right down the street, there's this large apartment house. I've contacted the owner. He's offered your wife a three-bedroom apartment for her and your daughter. When your house is sold, we'll move her over there. He will pay her $850 a month plus free utilities in return for which she can collect rents and supervise plumbing and electrical repair. She'll be there till your daughter graduates from high school, and the income from your house should pay for her college.'

> 📖 "'The final thing is, I've gotten a team of young men from the church who've volunteered to pool their money and rent a U-Haul truck and move her, so it won't cost her a cent.'
>
> 📖 "'I want you to be able to die in peace, knowing that your wife and daughter are cared for. One thing I need is your permission to execute these plans for you after you've gone.'
>
> 📖 "And Jack just cried like a baby."[51]

We shouldn't think that only Christians deserve our love. Whether they come to faith in Christ or not, we must do love to non-Christians as well.

We must not become disillusioned when we discover that our love is incomplete and flawed. Our re-birth did not make us perfect! But if we are ever to become witnessing Christians, we must grow in Christ-like love.

The role of reason

Many Christians have stumbled into the pit that says feelings (the emotions) are more reliable than reasoning (the intellect) to determine God's leading and will. If you have bought this line, it's past time you discarded it. God made us humans with both cognitive abilities and an emotive nature. Both have value; neither is infallible.

Jesus quoted the Old Testament when he said:

✝ *"Love the Lord your God with all your heart and with all your soul and with all your mind." (Matthew 22:37)*

Notice that Jesus included the mind. The Apostle Paul, under the inspiration of the Holy Spirit, wrote:

✒ *Do not conform any longer to the pattern of this world, but be transformed by the renewing of your mind. Then you will be able to test and approve what God's will is—his good, pleasing and perfect will. (Romans 12:2)*

And also:

✒ *But we have the mind of Christ. (1 Corinthians 2:16)*

Why would God want to transform our minds into the mind of Christ if we were not to use them? We should use our minds in worship, in earning a living, in recreation, in prayer, in relationships, in understanding our culture, and in witnessing. Do you doubt some

---

[51] Larry Richards and Paul Johnson, *Death and the Caring Community*, Multnomah Press, 1980, pp.45-46, 51-52.

of these? In 1 Corinthians 14:14, Paul said he would pray and sing to God with his mind—not just his spirit.[52] And the angel speaking to the writer of Revelation says that understanding the vision of the woman, beasts, horns, and the hills "calls for a mind with wisdom." (Revelation 17:9)

Being a Christian does not mean tossing your mind in the trashcan. Instead, it means that you should allow God to change it, you should train it, and you should use it to his glory. And if you did not know this, you need to get this permanently fixed deeply in your mindset now.

The role of the church

What part does the local church have in this divinely mandated endeavor? The church is not only a place to worship God, it is also where we are nurtured and protected by the community of faith. Part of this nurturing should be training to become Christ's ambassadors.

☞ *It was he [Christ] who gave some to be apostles, some to be prophets, some to be evangelists, and some to be pastors and teachers, to prepare God's people for works of service, so that the body of Christ may be built up until we all reach unity in the faith and in the knowledge of the Son of God and become mature, attaining to the whole measure of the fullness of Christ.*

Then we will no longer be infants, tossed back and forth by the waves, and blown here and there by every wind of teaching and by the cunning and craftiness of men in their deceitful scheming. Instead, speaking the truth in love, we will in all things grow up into him who is the Head, that is, Christ. From him the whole body, joined and held together by every supporting ligament, grows and builds itself up in love, as each part does its work. (Ephesians 4:11-16)

Christ raises up leadership in the church to equip us to do what God wants us to do—and this includes witnessing.

The church leadership should be using the Bible—not pop psychology or cultural leadership techniques—to help Christians learn how to allow the Holy Spirit to renew and transform our minds (Romans 12:2). Paul reminded Timothy of the usefulness of the Scriptures:

---

[52] Many interpret "spirit" in this verse to mean "emotions." What do you think?

🕊 *All Scripture is God-breathed and is useful for teaching, rebuking, correcting and training in righteousness, so that the man of God may be thoroughly equipped for every good work. (2 Timothy 3:16-17)*

And the good works we are being equipped to do includes witnessing. If your church is not using the Bible to prepare you to fulfill God's call on your life, you should either help the leadership change, or find a different church to go to.

Here are some important characteristics of a healthy church (and of a healthy Christian, too). A healthy church is:

- Bible based
- Christ-centered (not man-centered)
- Guided by the Spirit
- Authentic (vs. artificial)
- Compassionate
- Relevant
- Relational
- Missions minded
- Spiritual
- Lead by people who have gifts of leadership given by God

Notice that each of these characteristics is conducive to effective outreach. Find a church like this, become a functioning part of it, and grow in your faith.

What does a healthy church do? A healthy church:

- Worships Jesus Christ as God.
- Teaches the Bible.
- Equips Christians to serve God.
- Provides fellowship with other Christians.
- Disciplines, rebukes, and corrects members when needed.

Too many churches are failing to accomplish the biblical mandate. Instead they have fallen prey to "mission drift." Charles Conn illustrated this in his book, *Making It Happen.* He wrote:

📖 When I lived in Atlanta, several years ago, I noticed in the Yellow Pages, in the listing of restaurants, an entry for a place called Church of God Grill. The peculiar name aroused my curiosity and I dialed the number. A man answered with a cheery, "Hello! Church of God Grill!" I asked how his restaurant had been given such an unusual name, and he told me: "Well, we had a little mission down here, and we started selling chicken dinners after church on

> Sunday to help pay the bills. Well, people liked the chicken, and we did such a good business, that eventually we cut back on the church services. After a while we just closed down the church altogether and kept on serving the chicken dinners. We kept the name we started with, and that's Church of God Grill."[53]

The only reason I laughed when I read this was to keep from crying. Far too many churches, denominations, and individuals have, over time, drifted away from their biblical mission. And this is especially true when it comes to personal witnessing. Don't let it happen to you.

Ironically, most local churches play another role: mission field. Most churches have several members and/or regular attendees who have never experienced the rebirth. This was true when modernism was the prevailing worldview, and the shift to postmodernism has only amplified this problem. Earlier I referred to these people as "cultural christians."

One of the greatest challenges is to bring a non-Christian church member to faith in Christ. They know much *about* Christ Jesus, but they do not know him as Lord and Savior. They fit Paul's description of people who have "a form of godliness" but deny God the right to rule their lives. (2 Timothy 3:5)

The role of gospel literature

Did God use a salvation tract to bring you to himself? Do you know anyone brought to salvation through a tract? I do, but not many. I do not dismiss gospel tracts, but I think we must choose and use them carefully. Some gospel tracts caricaturize non-Christians as idiots—not exactly a relationship-building approach. Typically a tract is most effective when given to a person after an oral witness.

Perhaps the greatest value of a tract is that a person can take it with him or her and re-read it many times. So if they misunderstood some aspect of the gospel message, they have a chance to correct it. Also, they may put it aside, rediscover it later, and read it at a more opportune time.

---

[53] Charles Paul Conn, *Making It Happen.* Fleming H. Revell, 1981, p.95.

> ✐ A tract that I wrote and published on the Internet is included in the Appendix. Stop now and read "If 'Christ is the Answer,' What's the Question?" on page 159. Do you think it is useful for postmodern Westerners? Describe what you think is strong and weak about this tract. Do some tracts quickly become outdated?

You might want to try your hand at writing your own witnessing tract now. But even if you don't, why don't you try to make a list of elements you would want to include, and another list of things you would want to be certain to exclude. This would be a great learning experience for you—even better when done by a team of two or three people!

> ✐ Based on what you have learned so far, what kind of a tract do you think has the greatest potential to reach postmodernists?
>
> ✐ Analyze one or two of what your think are the very best tracts. What do you think makes them excellent? Describe any weaknesses.

Years ago while I was teaching at a state university, I often visited in a nursing home with a friend. John told me that he wanted me to meet a lady I'll call Theresa. I was completely unprepared for what I experienced!

Theresa was probably in her thirties and confined to a bed. She had no teeth and no control over her limbs or over her bodily functions. The nurses would feed her with a modified baby bottle and change her huge diaper as necessary. Daily they would move her to a wheelchair and secure her with a tied sheet.

I apologize if this sounds unloving, but I thought Theresa's physical appearance was one of the most repulsive I had ever seen. To make matters worse, I could not understand her speech. What a physically wretched creature!

John instructed her, "Tell Steve what you told me, Theresa." Then, after she said something, John asked me, "Did you understand her?" I was embarrassed, but I had to tell them I did not. This was repeated a few times before John told me, "She said, 'I love Jesus.'"

Then John showed me a small stack of tracts on the table beside her bed. A Christian nurse had taken the time to learn to understand Theresa's slurred speech and had used paper and pencil to write what Theresa told her to write. She helped Theresa save a few dollars every month and then took it all to a local printer. This tract had a photo of Theresa and her simple salvation testimony. And John told me that he knew of several people who had come to trust the Lord through this tract! Now, tell me again…why is it that you do not witness to friends?

> ✐ What effect does Theresa's story have on you? Does this story motivate you to use the abilities you have, or do you just bog down in guilt? Can you choose how you will react?

Characteristics of a good tract

Effective gospel tracts generally have these features:

- attractive, eye appeal
- brief and easy to read
- common language rather than church jargon
- explains the plight of humans as sinners
- clearly points to Jesus as the Savior
- fits the culture of the intended audience
- avoids peripheral issues
- calls for a response from the reader
- gives the name of a person or a church to contact

> ✐ Use these criteria above to evaluate two or three tracts.

Just as long as it works

What about our methods? Are there biblical and nonbiblical methods of witnessing and evangelism? Without question, any witness is wrong (unbiblical) if it includes either of these features:

- Saying anything inconsistent with God's character or Word.
- Doing anything inconsistent with God's character or Word.
- Distorting the gospel message in order to "win a convert."

Generally, I would say almost any method of witnessing that avoids these errors is acceptable. We're limited only by our imaginations and the leading of the Holy Spirit.

John Stackhouse describes the situation of the witnessing Christian and witnessing church succinctly:

> 📖 The challenge, then, is to complement our proclamation of the Gospel and our resistance to evil with winsome public demonstrations of God's care for the earth, for the financially and

socially needy, for beauty and joy and for the intellectual life. We must demonstrate our worthy citizenship if we are to overcome the plausibility problem today. The examples of Christian endeavor we have considered in this essay, then, can inspire us. And we must understand thereby that it is authentic for us to embrace this wide agenda, not just as something we "put on" strategically for the sake of evangelism but as cooperation with the God who is at work to redeem the whole world.[54]

At all costs we must avoid the pragmatism instilled in us by our culture. Some say, "You cannot argue with success." Yes we can—and we must. Our authority is the Scripture, not the world's definition of success.

---

[54] John G. Stackhouse, Jr., "From Architecture to Argument: Historic Resources for Christian Apologetics," in Timothy Phillips and Dennis Okholm, eds., *Christian Apologetics in the Postmodern World*, InterVarsity Press, pp.50-51.

*"Truth has perished; it has
vanished from their lips."*
Jeremiah 7:28

Chapter 6
Problems, Problems, Problems

The postmodern problem

Why is witnessing to postmodernists problematic? Why can't they be evangelized like our fathers and their fathers were? How are these people different? Carson describes the effect of postmodernism on witnessing:

> In any case, as much of Western culture increasingly distances itself from its Judeo-Christian roots, the task of evangelism takes on the overtones of a missionary enterprise to an alien culture: part of the task is bound up with understanding that culture.[55]

The primary problem is the rejection of all metanarratives by postmodernists; this is what makes witnessing to them difficult. Consider the effects the characteristics of postmodernism listed below have on attempting to communicate the Gospel.

Rampant relativism. Postmodernists see all truth as subjective. There are no absolutes, no objective Truth. Your religion is true for you, and mine is true for me. The Bible and its truth claims are all in doubt to them. This relativism promotes a pragmatism that says whatever works is right.

Deconstructed language. Deconstruction claims that words have no objective meaning or reality. This was discussed earlier in Chapter 1. If you have difficulty remembering what it is, reread it before continuing. This fallacious philosophical position is the foundation for the next characteristic.

Flawed hermeneutic. Even if you get a postmodernist to read a Bible text, he or she may use a different hermeneutic. They may well reject an approach that claims that the reader should strive to discover the intent of the original author and claim that the only meaning that matters is the meaning that the reader assigns it. I am confident that

---

[55] Carson, *The Gagging of God.* pp.491-492.

postmodernist writers would not be satisfied with a reader applying this same hermeneutic to their own writings.

Warped logic. Many postmodernists have discarded some of the rules of logic—specifically the law of non-contradiction. This says that two contradictory statements cannot both be true in the same sense. But some postmodernists reject this. How can you even hope to dialog with people who embrace such fallacious logic?

Biblical ignorance. Not only can you not assume people today believe the Bible, you also cannot assume people today know anything about the Bible, including the Bible stories you learned in Sunday school. And what they do know, they probably consider myth. So basing your witness on quoting the Bible is not necessarily a strength—you might merely appear naive, if not downright feeble-minded! And that is not likely to enhance your witness.

Popular fictions. Connected to this ignorance of what the Bible says is the fact that many non-Christians think the Bible says things that it does not say. "God helps those who help themselves" and "Cleanliness is next to godliness" immediately come to my mind as examples. Recently George Barna noted that American church members have a great deal of knowledge about what the Bible says, but that often their understanding of the meaning of the Bible is in error.[56]

The 19th Century American humorist Charles Farrar Browne (writing under the pseudonym Artemus Ward) is quoted as saying, "It ain't so much what people don't know that hurts as what they know that ain't so."[57] How true this is regarding popular misconceptions of what the Bible says.

Scientific imperialism. During the 1800s the natural sciences ascended to a leadership role in our culture. Throughout most of the 1900s, science reigned supreme as the arbiter of what constitutes knowledge or reality—not only in academia but also in the minds of the populace. This idea that only the scientific method can hope to arrive at truth has produced a worldview that claims the physical

---

[56] George Barna, "Americans' Bible Knowledge Is In the Ballpark, But Often Off Base," July 12, 2000, www.barna.org/cgi-bin/Home.asp.

[57] "Creative Quotations From…" www.bemorecreative.com/one/1839.htm. In *The Oxford Dictionary of Quotations* (p. 84), a variation of this statement is attributed to *Josh Billing's Encyclopedia of Wit and Wisdom*, 1874.

realm is all that exists (this is known as SCIENTISM). We should recognize scientism as based on faith in humans—our abilities to observe and to reason.

But the methods of science are crucially limited. As Jim Leffel told the faculty at Cornell University:

> 📖 We also recognize that science by its very nature lacks the capacity to provide a meaningful moral framework to apply its knowledge.[58]

So, while science may discover ways to perform safe abortions (well, safe for the mother, not for the baby!), it is powerless to help us discover if performing that abortion is right or wrong. The scientific method is amoral.[59] Alas, postmodernists sees all ethics as relative anyway.

Further, while postmodern Westerners typically care little for scientific knowledge, they love its sibling, technology. And they usually embrace "scientific conclusions" as weightier—when they want to. But, worse yet, many of them believe science has proven there is no God.

Intellectual inertia. Frankly, many who consider themselves atheists or AGNOSTICS are really just unwilling to do the work to analyze and evaluate the claims of Christianity. So our lives and conversation with them should stimulate them to overcome this inertia.

✐ Is it obvious to you how difficult it is to develop a winning strategy for sharing the Gospel with people who embrace this worldview? Pair up with a friend. One of you use the traits described above to play the part of a postmodernist, and the other attempt to witness to him or her. In your journal, make notes of your observations (1) of the problems you faced in witnessing and (2) of the frustrations you felt.

The problem of God's existence

Postmodernists typically deny that God exists. If there is no metanarrative, there can be no metanarrator (and vice versa). Others,

---

[58] Jim Leffel, "The New Challenge in Christian Apologetics." Presentation to Cornell University Faculty, April 1999, www.crossrds.org/cornell.htm.

[59] This is not the only limitation of the scientific method.

however, claim to be agnostics rather than atheists. In order to dialogue with these people effectively, you need to know why you believe in God.

What empirical evidence do you have for God's existence? Can a scientifically literate person believe in God and be rationally consistent? Of course, I answer that question affirmatively. (In case you did not know, my B.S. is in biology and my Ph.D. is in biochemistry. A brief biographical sketch is on page 183.)

> ✎ Have you ever tried to witness to someone who claimed to be an atheist? What approach did you take? What happened? How would you do that today? What would you change?

Many Christians have read or heard this: "The fool says in his heart, 'There is no God.'" (Psalm 14:1 and 53:1) Will quoting this to a Postmodern non-Christian help build a relationship of trust from which you can witness effectively?

> ✎ How do you think you could use this verse constructively in witnessing to a postmodernist?

Paul tells us one way that God has revealed himself to all people.

> ⚘ *The wrath of God is being revealed from heaven against all the godlessness and wickedness of men who suppress the truth by their wickedness, since what may be known about God is plain to them, because God has made it plain to them. For since the creation of the world God's invisible qualities—his eternal power and divine nature—have been clearly seen, being understood from what has been made, so that men are without excuse. (Romans 1:18-20)*

Perhaps Christians should be prepared to use this evidence of creation to help people understand God's power and nature.

What do think are the best evidences for God's existence? *Does God Exist?* is a book that presents a debate between a nonbeliever and a Christian.[60] Some time ago I tried to assemble my own list of evidences for a belief in God, and these are abridged for you in the Appendix ("How can a natural scientist be a Christian too?" page 161). It is not intended as a complete personal apologetic, just a set of

---

[60] J.P. Moreland and Kai Nielsen, *Does God exist?* Prometheus Books, 1993. Another good book is James Sire's *Why Should Anyone Believe Anything at All?* InterVarsity Press, 1994.

starting notes. You'll probably see some overlap between that short piece and this book.

> ✎ After reading my apologia, write your own "best evidence" for God's existence in your journal. What convinces you that God exists?

Have you ever taken the time to reflect on why you believe in Jesus? Or are you a bit timid to dwell on this question? If you hope to lead someone to believing in Jesus and accepting his rule, you must have a good idea of why *you* believe in Jesus and accept his reign in your life.

The problem of sin

Sin is the ultimate problem of all humans—and Jesus is the only solution. And, sooner or later, a person will have to deal with his or her own sinfulness if he or she is ever to recognize a personal need for the Savior. This is the problem we consider here.

If you comprehend the description of postmodernism, it should be clear why postmodernists would have difficulty seeing themselves as sinners. The very concept of sin is foreign to the postmodern mind—though an awareness of sin lurks in their being because they are made in God's image. So a clear and biblical definition of sin becomes crucial.

> ✎ Do you think someone could become a Christian without recognizing himself or herself as a sinner? Explain your answer. How would you try to convince someone who does not believe in sin that he or she is a sinner? Should you try to do this?

From its very beginning, the Bible shows how sin came into existence. Eve, then Adam, disobeyed God. The progressive revelation of the Old Testament tells the story of God's people, the children of Israel, passing through cycles of disobedience, judgment and punishment, repentance, God's deliverance and salvation, followed by disobedience again (e.g., the Book of Judges).

How does the New Testament describe sin? Consider these passages:

🕊 *All have sinned and fall short of the glory of God. (Romans 3:22-23)*

🕊 *Everything that does not come from faith is sin. (Romans 14:23)*

🕊 *Anyone, then, who knows the good he ought to do and doesn't do it, sins. (James 4:17)*

🕊 *Everyone who sins breaks the law...sin is lawlessness. (1 John 3:4)*

🕊 *All wrongdoing is sin. (1 John 5:17)*

Not only must people accept God's definition of sin, they must also recognize themselves as sinners who deserve God's judgment on sin. And God's just punishment for sin is death—everlasting separation from God.

So the Bible describes sin as universal, as not believing God, and as not obeying God. Further, if you think that you solve the problem by simply claiming there are no laws—well, as you just read, that is lawlessness, and that itself is sin.

The concept of humans as sinners has at least two meanings to most Evangelicals. First, we are sinners because we have inherited a sinful nature from Adam and Eve. Second, we are sinners because of our disbelief and disobedience to God. So the salvation that God offers us through Christ Jesus provides us both with forgiveness for the sinful acts we have done, and with a transformation of our sinful nature into a holy nature! This is the New Testament Gospel that we have to share with everyone.

Postmodernists have continued the process used by modernists of redefining sin as something else. This redefining process is illustrated by a sad personal experience. The *Pentecostal Evangel* published something I had written concerning what the Bible says about how Christians should respond to people who also claim to be Christians but who also live a sinful lifestyle (including homosexuality).[61] In that article, I had quoted part of Paul's instruction in 1 Corinthians 5:9-11:

🕊 *I have written you in my letter not to associate with sexually immoral people—not at all meaning the people of this world who are immoral, or the greedy and swindlers, or idolaters. In that case you would have to leave this world. But now I am writing you that you must not associate with anyone who calls himself a brother but is sexually immoral or greedy, an idolater or a slanderer, a drunkard or a swindler. With such a man do not even eat.*

---

[61] Steve Badger, "Letter to a Homosexual Friend," p.19 and "Guidelines for Being a Friend to a Homosexual," p.22. *Pentecostal Evangel.* Feb. 13, 2000. The *Pentecostal Evangel* is a magazine published weekly by the Assemblies of God.

This seems pretty straightforward. I cautioned Christians attempting to effectively witness to a homosexual that this text indicates that the day could come when they would have to end that friendship.

A few days after this was published, I received an unsigned letter from someone claiming to be a Christian leader in Tulsa who scolded me for my intolerance. Here is part of what he wrote:

> 📖 I have friends who are gay and Christian. Some of these followers of Jesus are currently involved in Assemblies of God churches, some partnered...some married to women and are bisexual. Some are in ministry positions—licensed and ordained...Some are celibate; some are not.

So in the name of tolerance, some would use a postmodernist hermeneutic and an illogical logic to twist the plain teaching of both the Old and New Testaments to accommodate the sins of their culture.

Others are suggesting homosexuality is genetically determined and, thus, not sin. Similarly, in his cover story article in Time (Aug. 15, 1994, p.44) "Our Changing Hearts," Robert Wright reports that evolutionary psychologists see humans as having a proclivity to sexual promiscuity. He writes:

> 📖 According to evolutionary psychologists, our everyday, ever shifting attitudes toward a mate or prospective mate—trust, suspicion, rhapsody, revulsion, warmth, iciness—are the handiwork of natural selection that remain with us today because in the past they led to behaviors that helped spread genes.[62]

If a person has a genetic predisposition (or evolutionary proclivity) for adultery, lying, or stealing, does that mean these are also not sin? Of course not! And no genetic discovery can ever change God's condemnation of homosexuality as sin in the Bible either. I also believe that if it is ever established that humans have a genetic predisposition for sexual promiscuity or homosexuality, it is not the result of God's perfect and good creation, but a consequence of the Fall (Adam and Eve's sin).

Unmarried couples who claim to be Bible-believing Christians but who are living together exemplify another similar form of cognitive dissonance. They fail to acknowledge the contradiction between their lives and the clear teaching of Scripture.

---

[62] Robert Wright, "Our Changing Hearts." *Time* August 15, 1994, p.46.

The problem of syncretism

Is it acceptable to join beliefs and practices from other religions to Christianity? According to the Bible, absolutely not! This is SYNCRETISM, and it must be avoided at all costs.

On the other hand, can we—should we—present the message in such a way that people of a given language and culture will find it most understandable? Many witnessing Christians answer this question "Yes," and we call it CONTEXTUALIZATION. Consider this example.

> In his Alaskan travels John Muir came across an Indian tribe that had eagerly accepted Christianity. When Muir inquired as to why they had been so receptive, he was told a fascinating story. About twenty or thirty years earlier there had been a particularly bitter war with a neighboring tribe. The battles never ended because each victory brought a fresh retaliation; the scores were never settled.

> After an unusually difficult summer of fighting, this tribe sent a delegation to its neighbors. "Look," they said, "winter will soon be here and we have had no time to gather our food. We are all facing starvation if we do not stop our fighting."

> "We cannot stop," the neighbors responded. "You have killed ten more men than we have; give us ten of your men and we will make peace." At that point one of the delegation spoke up. "You know that I am the chief of our tribe. I am worth ten men. Kill me so that the score can be equaled and the fighting stopped." So they did. In the presence of all the people, the chief was put to death. And the fighting stopped. When shortly after this the missionary came and explained the meaning of Christ's death, the response was immediate and lasting, as even an unbeliever like John Muir was forced to notice.[63]

Perhaps this missionary connected the Gospel to their experience, or perhaps the people did this for themselves. Paul's sermon in Athens could be cited as another example:

> *Paul then stood up in the meeting of the Areopagus and said: "Men of Athens! I see that in every way you are very religious. For as I walked around and looked carefully at your objects of worship, I even found an altar with this inscription: To An Unknown God. Now*

---

[63] As quoted by William Dyrness, *How Does America Hear the Gospel?* William B. Eerdmans, 1989, pp.10-11.

what you worship as something unknown I am going to proclaim to you. (Acts 17:22-23)

He began his proclamation of the Gospel with something they knew and understood. Of course, it was inadequate, and he had to leave it behind and preach the resurrection of Christ Jesus—but he tried to accommodate the Athenians by beginning with a part of their culture with which they could identify. It gained Paul a hearing, and some of them wanted to hear Paul again, and others believed.

The first chapter of Don Richardson's *Eternity in Their Hearts* describes the history behind this event in Acts 17 in some detail. Some people see Don Richardson's book *Peace Child* as an example of contextualizing the Gospel for a culture. (You may wish to get either book from the library.)

What is the point of all this? In your witnessing, use cultural connections as hooks to connect the hearer to the message. But as you attempt to present the Gospel in ways that the lost can understand and receive the message, you must never distort the gospel message to dilute or weaken it or make it more acceptable!

We have no warrant to change the Gospel in any way. The Gospel is God's unilateral offer. It is completely non-negotiable. And the genuine Gospel of Christ Jesus will never be culturally acceptable—if you succeed in making it so, it will not be the real thing, and what you have left will be robbed of its power to change lives!

Most Christians easily spot syncretism in Christians who live in other cultures, but, to my great dismay, they are completely blind to their own syncretistic practices. I'm forced to assume I have similar blind spots.

> ✎ Try to identify the cultural baggage we have in our Western brands of Christianity. You might consider things like our forms of worship, our church structures, and our approaches to work, recreation, money, and authority.

The problem of rejection and failure

Several years ago a young Christian and I were praying together at dusk on a college campus. At the end of our prayer, I told Randy that I felt that the Holy Spirit was leading me to walk a couple of blocks to Bob's apartment, perhaps to encourage him. We could stay only a few minutes, but Randy agreed to go with me.

When we got there, Bob introduced us to a young man I'll call Dick. After several minutes of friendly conversation, I asked Dick if anyone had ever talked with him about Jesus. Our conversation quickly went from bad to worse, and Dick suddenly became extremely hostile, using vulgar—almost violent—language to reject my attempts to tell him of the Lord.

A few minutes later, as we were walking back to the campus, Randy said to me, "Boy, you really blew it."

"Why do you say that?" I asked.

"Well, because of the way Dick reacted. Obviously, you were not following the leading of the Holy Spirit, or he would not have reacted to you that way."

✎ Do you agree with Randy's assessment of my attempt to witness to Dick? Explain why, and if possible, use examples from the New Testament to support your ideas.

Almost every Christian who has ever witnessed for the Savior has experienced rejection and felt like a failure. But not all who hear the Gospel receive it. Some reject it, and some react quite aggressively. Paul's experiences in Athens and in Ephesus illustrate this quite well (Acts 17 and 19). Jesus told his disciples to remember this:

✞ *"'No servant is greater than his master.' If they persecuted me, they will persecute you also." (John 15:20)*

There is more to this story. About a year later a visitor came to a Thursday night prayer meeting at my house. He introduced himself to me and reminded me that I had tried to witness to him one night, but he would not let me. But, he said, God had used that to start him thinking about his life and about God, and just a few days earlier, he had confessed his sins and placed his faith in Jesus. That stranger was Dick.

All experiences will not end this way, but just a few should serve to remind us that our task is to live a holy life and tell others of the Savior. What looks like failure today may be seen as success sometime later. We need to learn how to leave the results up to God.

The problem of our lack of knowledge

One of the biggest obstacles to Christians witnessing is our lack of biblical knowledge. We often do not know what orthodox Christian

(Bible) doctrine is. We often do not know *why* we believe what we believe. And so we lack confidence in a discussion—even less in a friendly debate.

We know we will appear ignorant, because we are. What is the solution to this problem? Our churches need to do better jobs of teaching believers the Word. Christians need to become more committed to learning biblical content. Small group interactions like Sunday school and home Bible studies are effective in developing a working knowledge of what the Bible teaches, and churches need to find other effective venues.

The more you know about what the Bible says, the more easily you can witness with confidence. But our ignorance goes beyond an ignorance of the Scriptures. We often appear ignorant in other ways too. When Christians appear ignorant about the things everyone knows, and then proclaim the Gospel, people assume their faith is as moronic as their general knowledge. This is not a new observation. St. Augustine addressed this situation about sixteen centuries ago.

> Usually, even a non-Christian knows something about the earth, the heavens, and the other elements of this world, about the motion and orbit of the stars and even their size and relative positions, about the predictable eclipses of the sun and moon, the cycles of the years and the seasons, about the kinds of animals, shrubs, stones, and so forth, and this knowledge he holds to as being certain from reason and experience. Now, it is a disgraceful and dangerous thing for an infidel to hear a Christian, presumably giving the meaning of Holy Scripture, talking nonsense on these topics; and we should take all means to prevent such an embarrassing situation, in which people show up vast ignorance in a Christian and laugh it to scorn. The shame is not so much that an ignorant individual is derided, but that people outside the household of the faith think our sacred writers held such opinions, and, to the great loss of those for whose salvation we toil, the writers of our Scripture are criticized and rejected as unlearned men. If they find a Christian mistaken in a field which they themselves know well and hear him maintaining his foolish opinions about our books, how are they going to believe those books in matters concerning the resurrection of the dead, the hope of eternal life, and the kingdom of heaven, when they think their pages are full of falsehoods on facts which they themselves have learnt from experience and the light of reason? Reckless and incompetent expounders of Holy Scripture bring untold trouble and

> sorrow on their wiser brethren when they are caught in one of their mischievous false opinions and are taken to task by those who are not bound by the authority of our sacred books. For then, to defend their utterly foolish and obviously untrue statements, they will try to call upon Holy Scripture for proof and even recite from memory many passages which they think support their position, although *they understand neither what they say nor the things about which they make assertion.*[64]

This is especially applicable when Christians witness to people who are scientifically literate. So we must not only be students of the Word of God, we must also be students of our culture and of the people to whom we hope to communicate the Gospel of Christ Jesus.

The problem of exclusivism

You have already seen that postmodernists see Christians as intolerant because we claim that Christianity is the only true faith. This exclusivity is the scandal of Christianity, and especially in our culture, where pluralism is the order of the day! Without a doubt, this is a problem that must be understood and addressed.

On May 12, 2000, the popular ABC news magazine show *20/20* had a story about a Baptist church in Dallas converting a 12-year-old Jewish boy. The Baptists were presented as wrongly intolerant because they claimed the Jewish religion was inadequate and that Christianity is the only true faith. Here is a quote from that story:

> 📖 The Roman Catholic Church, the United Methodist Church and the Presbyterian Church all strongly discourage conversion of Jews to Christianity and encourage interfaith dialogue. And many Christian denominations, including moderate Baptists and Roman Catholics, the largest Christian denomination in the United States, say they believe one can get to heaven without believing in Jesus.[65]

I am not defending this Baptist church's methods here—I'm not even sure what they were. But if Jesus and Peter were right (John 14:6

---

[64] Augustine, *St. Augustine: The Literal Meaning of Genesis*, Vol. I, Books 1-6, Quasten and others, eds., translated and annotated by John Hammond Taylor, S. J. Ancient Christian Writers: The Works of the Fathers in Translation, No. 41, Newman Press, 1982, pp.42-43. Italics in the original.

[65] "Converting a Child," abcnews.go.com/onair/2020/2020_000512_conversion_feature.html.

and Acts 4:12), this Jewish boy's only hope of eternity is the same as yours and mine: the atoning death of Christ Jesus.

Prof. Charles Hedrick solves this problem of exclusivism with a postmodern conclusion (see his essay mentioned earlier on page 6). Hedrick argues that every Christian group considers their church the only orthodox church; then he concludes:

> All of this raises the question: are there no absolutes in religion? Of course there are! Just ask the Baptists, the Roman catholics [sic] and the Orthodox.[66]

In other words, Hedrick is (derisively) answering the question of the existence of absolute religious truth with a decided, "No."

> Explain why many assert that the statement "There are no absolute truths" is self-refuting. Can you think of any other examples of self-refuting statements?

The problem of truth: testing truth claims

Postmodernists claim there is no such thing as truth. But, as noted earlier, this statement is self-refuting—the statement itself is a truth claim. Some of them would challenge us with "Who is to say what truth is?" The answer is "Each one of us should use our God-given abilities to try to determine truth."

How have people tested truth claims through the centuries? I'll try to avoid a boring or complex philosophical treatise here, so let me just summarize a few tests.

Correspondence. This approach says that truth corresponds to the reality we observe in the world. If your friend tells you she is healthy, but she has a fever and is so dizzy she cannot walk without your help, you conclude her statement is not true because it does not correspond to your observation.

Coherence. A truth claim cannot be self-contradictory or self-refuting. It must "hang together" as a whole.

Consistent. We usually doubt a truth claim if it is inconsistent with other truth claims that we are confident are true.

Definitions. Finally, some truth claims are really just definitions. Bachelors are unmarried, for example, is merely a definition.

---

[66] Hedrick, "True Religion? It All Depends." *Springfield News-Leader.* July 10, 2000, p.8A.

Authority. Some people have experiences, training, and/or education that makes them knowledgeable in a particular field. You embrace this theory of truth every time you go to the dentist or a physician and every time you take your ailing automobile to a mechanic. You recognize that they are authorities in their fields.

How can we apply these tests to our Christian faith? Christians generally find that the Bible passes the test of correspondence, the test of coherence, and the test of consistency. We sometimes work to grasp biblical definitions of words (i.e., justification, sin, heaven, and hell).

Probably one of the most difficult and significant tests is that of authority. In Matthew 28:18, Jesus said, "All authority in heaven and on earth has been given to me." If the God of the Bible exists, he alone is authoritative—and any record of what God said would also be authoritative.

Fundamental to our task is the fact that postmodernists generally reject these tests of truth claims. These are all Modernist tests. Christians need to learn how to demonstrate to open-minded people that there are some absolute truths. Our goal, then, is to help non-Christians see the value of some truth claims, and then to see that Christianity passes these tests.

The problem of relatives

For many Christians who witness regularly, their biggest problem is witnessing effectively to their kin. Parents, siblings, children, and other relatives know us so well, we fear they will doubt the sincerity of our witness or the reality of our conversion. But nowhere does the Bible hint we can ignore our families.

When God described the fast he had chosen for his people in Isaiah 58, he said "not to turn away from your own flesh and blood" (58:7). Then in 1 Timothy 5:8, Paul wrote:

> *If anyone does not provide for his relatives, and especially for his immediate family, he has denied the faith and is worse than an unbeliever.*

If this is true concerning physical needs, how much more is it true for spiritual needs that will determine eternal destiny?

Secular people

Worldviews tend to produce people with certain characteristics, and our current postmodern culture is certainly no exception. George Hunter says secular people are "not, by and large, a-religious, immoral, or sophisticated."[67] He describes them in this way. Secular people:

- 📖 Are essentially ignorant of basic Christianity.
- 📖 Are seeking life *before* death.
- 📖 Are conscious of doubt more than guilt.
- 📖 Have a negative image of the Church.
- 📖 Have multiple alienations.
- 📖 Are untrusting.
- 📖 Have low self-esteem.
- 📖 Experience forces in history as "out of control."
- 📖 Experience forces in personality as "out of control."
- 📖 Cannot find "the door."[68]

However, we must not think that all secular people have all of these characteristics. These are generalizations that may give us insights.

Now that we better understand these secular postmodernists and how they think, God can help us to develop strategies for reaching them with the Gospel.

---

[67] George Hunter, *How to Reach Secular People.* Abingdon Press, 1992, p.43.
[68] Hunter, pp.44-54.

Now these things occurred as examples...
1 Corinthians 10:6

Chapter 7
Learn From Good Fishermen

Two early witnesses

John the Baptist was the first to publicly identify the adult Jesus as "the Lamb of God, who takes away the sin of the world." (John 1:29) Andrew was the second. Study this passage and see what you can learn about witnessing.

> *The next day John was there again with two of his disciples. When he saw Jesus passing by, he said, "Look, the Lamb of God!"*
>
> *When the two disciples heard him say this, they followed Jesus. Turning around, Jesus saw them following and asked, "What do you want?"*
>
> *They said, "Rabbi" (which means Teacher), "where are you staying?"*
>
> *"Come," he replied, "and you will see."*
>
> *So they went and saw where he was staying, and spent that day with him. It was about the tenth hour.*
>
> *Andrew, Simon Peter's brother, was one of the two who heard what John had said and who had followed Jesus. The first thing Andrew did was to find his brother Simon and tell him, "We have found the Messiah." And he brought him to Jesus. (John 1:35-42)*

✎ Can we use this or other New Testament texts to discover a biblical pattern for evangelism or witnessing? How did Andrew respond to John's identification of Jesus? What did Andrew do after spending time with Jesus? How can you apply this to your witnessing today?

Illustrations from Acts

Luke's Acts is the only biblical account we have of the church in its infancy. So let's examine it to see what we can learn about how God used people to spread the Gospel.

Acts 2 records the exciting Day of Pentecost when Peter preached and 3,000 people were saved! Acts 7 records Stephen's witness and the reaction of the people—they stoned him to death. But I suspect that Saul, who was present, in witnessing this was prepared for his conversion.

The example of Philip witnessing to the Ethiopian eunuch is a great example because it illustrates several things.

✍ *Now an angel of the Lord said to Philip, "Go south to the road—the desert road—that goes down from Jerusalem to Gaza." So he started out, and on his way he met an Ethiopian eunuch, an important official in charge of all the treasury of Candace, queen of the Ethiopians. This man had gone to Jerusalem to worship, and on his way home was sitting in his chariot reading the book of Isaiah the prophet. The Spirit told Philip, "Go to that chariot and stay near it."*

Then Philip ran up to the chariot and heard the man reading Isaiah the prophet. "Do you understand what you are reading?" Philip asked.

"How can I," he said, "unless someone explains it to me?" So he invited Philip to come up and sit with him.

The eunuch was reading this passage of Scripture:

"He was led like a sheep to the slaughter, and as a lamb before the shearer is silent, so he did not open his mouth. In his humiliation he was deprived of justice. Who can speak of his descendants? For his life was taken from the earth."

The eunuch asked Philip, "Tell me, please, who is the prophet talking about, himself or someone else?" Then Philip began with that very passage of Scripture and told him the good news about Jesus.

As they traveled along the road, they came to some water and the eunuch said, "Look, here is water. Why shouldn't I be baptized?" And he gave orders to stop the chariot. Then both Philip and the eunuch went down into the water and Philip baptized him. (Acts 8:26-38)

🖊 Before you read on, make notes on what you see as exemplary in this passage. In what ways was Philip a good witness? Don't read ahead to see what I think!

Notice that God (an angel and the Holy Spirit) directed Philip. He initiated a conversation based on where the man was and what he was doing at that moment. And, even though their meeting was brief, they quickly established some kind of a relationship of trust. He used the Old Testament to explain how Jesus fulfilled the prophecy—but Philip *told him the good news of Jesus*!

The conversion of Saul (Acts 9) illustrates the power of the Holy Spirit and the sovereignty of God. Later in chapter 9, God used Peter in Joppa to raise a beloved lady, Dorcas, from the dead. The result?

✣ *This became known all over Joppa, and many people believed in the Lord. (Acts 9:42)*

So a manifestation of the power of the Holy Spirit was evangelistic.

Although the story of Peter and Cornelius may primarily be there to teach everyone that God sent his salvation to all humans and not just to the Jews, the account also illustrates a good witness: the Holy Spirit and the Scriptures were both key. But examine Luke's summary of Peter's witness to Cornelius:

✣ *Then Peter began to speak: "I now realize how true it is that God does not show favoritism but accepts men from every nation who fear him and do what is right. You know the message God sent to the people of Israel, telling the good news of peace through Jesus Christ, who is Lord of all. You know what has happened throughout Judea, beginning in Galilee after the baptism that John preached—how God anointed Jesus of Nazareth with the Holy Spirit and power, and how he went around doing good and healing all who were under the power of the devil, because God was with him.*

"We are witnesses of everything he did in the country of the Jews and in Jerusalem. They killed him by hanging him on a tree, but God raised him from the dead on the third day and caused him to be seen. He was not seen by all the people, but by witnesses whom God had already chosen—by us who ate and drank with him after he rose from the dead. He commanded us to preach to the people and to testify that he is the one whom God appointed as judge of the living and the dead. All the prophets testify about him that everyone who believes in him receives forgiveness of sins through his name."

While Peter was still speaking these words, the Holy Spirit came on all who heard the message. The circumcised believers who had come with Peter were astonished that the gift of the Holy Spirit had been poured out even on the Gentiles. For they heard them speaking in tongues and praising God.

Then Peter said, "Can anyone keep these people from being baptized with water? They have received the Holy Spirit just as we have." So he ordered that they be baptized in the name of Jesus Christ. Then they asked Peter to stay with them for a few days. (Acts 10:34-48)

Notice how Peter proclaimed the death and resurrection of Jesus. But also notice how the Holy Spirit confirmed and validated Peter's words!

Finally, when Paul witnessed to Festus and Agrippa (in Acts 26:24-29), Festus thought too much education had driven Paul mad (students, can you identify?). Agrippa asked Paul "Do you think that in such a short time you can persuade me to be a Christian?" (v.28) Do you suppose Paul would have answered "Yes" or "No"? Postmodernists today often think Christians are crazy—but not because of too much education.

Old Testament examples

The Bible has many examples of God's people living in pagan cultures. Joseph was sold into slavery in Egypt, and Moses grew up there. The children of Israel lived in exile in Babylon, and some of God's greatest prophets—like Daniel and Ezekiel—lived in this foreign culture.

But the record of their lives and experiences does not give us too many specific instructions for witnessing to people in a different culture. Perhaps the biggest point is this: Be faithful to God wherever you live.

Biblical patterns

I think a couple of sentences in the passage we read earlier from the first chapter of John give us insights into witnessing. Let me rewrite it with emphasis for you. The **first thing** Andrew did was to **find** his brother Simon and **tell him**, "We have found the Messiah"...And he **brought him to Jesus**.

Of course this was all predicated on Andrew having spent time with Jesus. But it was a "first thing" *priority*; he had to *find* Simon; then he *told* him what he'd experienced; then he *brought* Simon to Jesus. Every Christian should be able to do this with a friend.

> ✐ Look at this from another perspective. What part of this is missing in your life? Is witnessing not a "first thing" priority? Are you unwilling to search for the lost? Does a verbal witness trouble you? Can you bring someone to Jesus?

The book of Acts provides insights into a biblical pattern of influence. Consider the use of the word "household" in these passages: Acts 11:14; 16:15; 16:31; and 18:8. The household was not restricted to the nuclear family, but included more distant relatives and servants. We can think of our "household" as those with whom we spend time, those with whom have some influence, and who have some influence in our lives. Remember this because we will develop this idea in Chapter 12.

Finally, from Acts we learn about the work of the Holy Spirit and the use of the Scriptures in witnessing. We cannot hope to fulfill the Great Commission without the power of the Holy Spirit and knowledge of the Word of God.

And the Old Testament provides us with the biblical worldview that provides the right grid for understanding who we are, who Christ is, and what he has done for us.

Why can't they see?

The Scriptures help us to understand why postmodernists cannot see the truth of the Gospel. Only the power of the Holy Spirit— usually expressed in the life of a believer—can open the eyes of these people. Can such a person stand before God's judgment throne and plead ignorance? Could a person legitimately say, "I would have believed in you, God, but there just wasn't any evidence"? Again Paul wrote:

> *The wrath of God is being revealed from heaven against all the godlessness and wickedness of men who suppress the truth by their wickedness, since what may be known about God is plain to them, because God has made it plain to them. For since the creation of the world God's invisible qualities—his eternal power and divine nature— have been clearly seen, being understood from what has been made, so that men are without excuse. For although they knew God, they neither glorified him as God nor gave thanks to him, but their thinking became futile and their...hearts were darkened. (Romans 1:18-21)*

So the creation itself bears witness to the fact of the Creator, and this revelation may be something we can use in witnessing.

Mildred Savage described a safety sign in a research laboratory:

- 📖 YOU CAN WALK WITH A WOODEN LEG
- 📖 YOU CAN EAT WITH FALSE TEETH
- 📖 BUT YOU CAN'T SEE WITH A GLASS EYE [69]

Perhaps postmodernists cannot see the truth of the Gospel because they are looking with glass eyes. Or to put this in biblical language:

The god of this age has blinded the minds of unbelievers, so that they cannot see the light of the gospel...of Christ (2 Corinthians 4:4)

If we are to become effective "fishers-of-men" we will have to become so knowledgeable of the Scriptures and of our culture—and so perfectly led by the Holy Spirit—that we can demonstrate and communicate God's offer of forgiveness—even to the blind!

---

[69] Mildred Savage, *In Vivo*. Simon and Schuster, 1964, p.17.

*Do your best to present yourself to God as...a workman
who...correctly handles the word of truth.*
2 Timothy 2:15

Chapter 8
Don't You Love It When a Plan Comes Together?

The place for conversion

Where should people come to faith in Jesus Christ? That sounds like a silly question. Is there a wrong place to get saved? The answer to my question might inform our thinking about strategies for witnessing.

If most Christians have any strategy for bringing the lost to Christ, it seems to be this: "Take them to church." So my question is really this: Is the New Testament pattern of witnessing "Invite them to the assembly of believers to hear the Gospel"?

I suggest the answer to this question is "No." Rather the New Testament model is one of people living their faith and sharing their experiences with the Savior to family and friends. (I offer this only as a typical pattern, not as a hard fast rule.) This may take place with one or two people (e.g., Philip and the Ethiopian eunuch) or with a group of people (e.g., Peter to Cornelius's household).

Some may object to this position by reminding us that on the Day of Pentecost Peter preached to the crowd and 3,000 came to faith. But this was "street-preaching," not a church meeting. Others may cite Romans 10:14-15:

⬦ *How, then, can they call on the one they have not believed in? And how can they believe in the one of whom they have not heard? And how can they hear without someone preaching to them? And how can they preach unless they are sent?*

What is the range of meaning of the Greek word translated *preach* and *preacher* here? This word refers to anyone who proclaims the Gospel, whether he or she is a professional minister or not. So in this sense, anyone who tells of God's offer of forgiveness is a preacher and is preaching.

There are some biblical exceptions to this generality, I admit, but I believe the typical New Testament pattern is personal witnessing.

> ✎ Make notes on the advantages and disadvantages of each of these two witnessing approaches: (1) Taking people to a church service to get saved; and, (2) Individual Christians witnessing in their homes, at work, and at school—in the marketplace.

Patterns of relationships

Christians today seem to live in relationship to non-Christians in one of three ways. Some isolate themselves from the lost as if they have a contagious illness. The QUMRAN COMMUNITY did this and abandoned all hope of influencing their culture. Others become all but indistinguishable from the non-Christian world by adapting to the cultural norms. For example, the Sadducees so accommodated themselves to the Greco-Roman culture that they had no witness.

But neither isolation nor compromise is biblical. Instead, the Bible instructs believers to live a holy, morally pure life while we minister to the lost within the context of our cultural grid. This is our goal:

🕊 *Since we have these promises, dear friends, let us purify ourselves from everything that contaminates body and spirit, perfecting holiness out of reverence for God. (2 Corinthians 7:1)*

🕊 *I have written you in my letter not to associate with sexually immoral people—not at all meaning the people of this world who are immoral, or the greedy and swindlers, or idolaters. In that case you would have to leave this world. (1 Corinthians 5:9-10)*

🕊 *Though I am free and belong to no man, I make myself a slave to everyone, to win as many as possible. To the Jews I became like a Jew, to win the Jews. To those under the law I became like one under the law (though I myself am not under the law), so as to win those under the law. To those not having the law I became like one not having the law (though I am not free from God's law but am under Christ's law), so as to win those not having the law. To the weak I became weak, to win the weak. I have become all things to all men so that by all possible means I might save some. (1 Corinthians 9:19-22)*

One of the most difficult challenges we Christians face is how we can be in the world, but not compromised—separated from the world, but not isolated from the lost we wish to win.

Why should people believe?

Have you ever taken the time to reflect on why you believe in Jesus? Or are you a bit timid to dwell on this question? James Sire offers five groups of reasons why people should believe Christianity is true (and offers a short bibliography of books that help to support his answers).

- The character of Jesus Christ as presented in the Gospels.
- The historical reliability of the Gospels.
- The internal consistency and coherence of the Christian worldview.
- The witness of the Church through the ages.
- The testimony of its [contemporary] adherents. [70]

> ✎ Do you recall how God convinced you of your need and his offer of forgiveness? If so, write some of these down to share with others.

Strategies for witnessing

As we consider what strategies could be most useful to reach postmodernists, we should reflect on the basic needs of all people. People long for the benefits that faith in Christ Jesus provides, including:

- A grid for making sense of our world.
- A basis for morality that gives meaning and dignity to our existence.
- A vision for life and a hope for eternity.
- The satisfaction of the deepest human need—reconciliation to the Creator. [71]

No single strategy for witnessing will work in every situation. This is true for every day and age. As the Apostle Paul traveled on his missionary trips, he had a pattern too.

> ✝ *As his custom was, Paul went into the synagogue, and on three Sabbath days he reasoned with them from the Scriptures, explaining and proving that the Christ had to suffer and rise from the dead. "This Jesus I am proclaiming to you is the Christ," he said. (Acts 17:2-3)*

---

[70] James Sire, "Why Should Anyone Believe Anything at All?" in *Telling the Truth* ed. by D. A. Carson, Zondervan, 2000, pp.100-101.

[71] This list is based on McGrath's *Intellectuals Don't Need God & Other Modern Myths*. pp.178-179.

Sometimes this worked better than other times. It seemed to work better in Iconium (Acts 14:1-4) than in Thessalonica (Acts 17:1-9). This often caused such problems with the Jews that Paul was forced to take the Gospel to the Gentiles (non-Jews).

Similarly, the strategies that built big churches across America in the '50s and '60s will not necessarily work in the 21st Century. A strategy that will work in the Midwest may not work in southern California or the Northeast. So what must we do?

Preparation to witness

Almost everything we do that is worthwhile requires preparation, and personal witnessing is no exception. This idea is developed more fully in the next chapter, but let me introduce it to you here. In order to be more effective witnesses, we must become students who constantly study and analyze:

1. God's Word and what it says.
2. Your world (including culture) and how it is changing.
3. How people communicate (language).
4. How people in our culture typically think and feel.

We can then apply this knowledge to communicating the lost condition of humankind, the consequences of our sin, and God's gracious offer of salvation. And there is no simple method or formula for applying this to all of the people you will meet in the years to come. Instead you must learn all you can, practice using everything you know, and practice following the leading of the Holy Spirit to lead someone to the same Savior who saved you.

If you are a college student, consider the courses that inform you about each of these four areas named above:

Area 1: God's Word	Area 2: Your World
All Bible courses, Greek, Hebrew, hermeneutics, HOMILETICS, & theology	History, sociology, science, physical education, philosophy, cross-cultural communications, missions, & music

Area 3: Communication, language	Area 4: People
English, literature, speech, drama, hermeneutics, homiletics, music, communications, philosophy, cross-cultural communications, & foreign languages	Philosophy, psychology, counseling, social science, ANTHROPOLOGY, and missions

Regardless of your major area of study, if you will view all of your learning and studying as preparation for witnessing, you should be more highly motivated in the courses that you don't particularly like.

As we attempt new methods of outreach, we must always be prepared to modify them. Our methods are not necessarily sacred; God's Word is sacred. Some may interrupt here and say, "God has chosen preaching as the method of spreading the Gospel." In fact, Paul wrote,

✝ *It pleased God by the foolishness of preaching to save them that believe. (1 Corinthians 1:21)*

But does this mean that preaching is the only way to spread the Gospel? Perhaps other parts of the New Testament can inform our thinking? In Acts 3, God used a healing event as a witness. In Acts 4, God continued to use that event to have Peter and John witness to the Sanhedrin. If you think this was just a special form of preaching, consider Philip and the Ethiopian eunuch in Acts 8.

Please do not misunderstand me. I wholeheartedly endorse evangelistic preaching! But it is not a substitute for individual Christians witnessing. Too often preaching is clouded by Christian culture and Christian jargon, both of which are foreign to non-Christians. In any case, it is not a case of "either one or the other," but of using both evangelistic preaching and personal witnessing! Also, in the assembly, the Christians need to be fed, not to be preached to as if they're lost.

So, our goal is to continually find ways to present the Gospel to the lost and unchurched in creative and effective ways. Our target audience is made up of postmodern non-Christians. We should prayerfully try to allow God's Holy Spirit to lead us in developing new approaches and strategies that will be more effective in reaching our target audience.

> ✎ List specific ways you have attempted witnessing in the past—whether by yourself or in a group. How did these attempts work? How did you feel afterwards? Would you want to use these methods again? How would you change them?

Faith? Or Reason?

The way some Christians have been presenting the Gospel and teaching converts about the Christian faith for at least the past several decades tends to work against effective witnessing. These Christians see Christianity as a matter of faith alone—to the exclusion of reason. Steve Zeisler said it this way:

> 📖 Simply stated, this tension is between an approach to God that is essentially rational, one in which we expect God to instruct our minds and we respond in obedience to what he tells us to do, and an approach...in which God's actions bypass our minds and we encounter him in unexpected and dramatic ways...These two different approaches to God do not need to come into conflict but, unfortunately, they often seem to do so.[72]

Postmodernists typically denigrate reason. But Jesus reasoned with the Jewish leaders. And in Acts 17 Paul "reasoned" with the Jews in Thessalonica. And this is not the only place we see this—this was Paul's pattern! Look at his activities in Acts 17:17 at Athens, in Acts 18:4 at Corinth, and in Acts 18:19 at Ephesus.

McCallum answers the question of faith or reason like this:

> 📖 Head-knowledge *can* puff up, as Paul warns in 1 Corinthians 8:1. And we need to reflect on the role of experience, both negative and positive, in the Christian life. These points we don't question. The real problem comes when heart-knowledge and head-knowledge are viewed from an "either-or" perspective instead of a "both-and" perspective. Such a division between our "hearts" and our "heads" is dangerous. What we know in our heads and our hearts should be *the same, not different.* Head-knowledge and heart-knowledge must always be compatible. Neither is

---

[72] Steve Zeisler, "Mind and Spirit," www.pbc.org/dp/zeisler/4075.html. Peninsula Bible Church of Palo Alto, California.

dispensable. Those who wish to deprecate one or the other create a dreadful caricature of real biblical Christianity.[73]

Asking if Christianity is based on faith or reason is what we call a false dichotomy. As McCallum said, we should not ask which one is more important. We must *have* and *use* both faith and reason. Each has its role, and excluding either is a mistake.

In Isaiah 1:18, God invites his sinful people with these words,

> *"Come now, let us reason together," says the LORD. "Though your sins are like scarlet, they shall be as white as snow; though they are red as crimson, they shall be like wool."*

God wants to reason with us. And we can use reason with others to help them consider the truth claims of Christ.

Dialogue includes listening

If you would share the Gospel with any person, you must first learn who he or she is, what his or her unique needs and experiences are. Unfortunately, many Christians have not learned to listen well. But you can learn how to listen, and your friends can help you learn too. Ask a close friend to candidly evaluate your listening skills. Discipline yourself to minimize your portion of the conversation.

Developing your listening skills is important, not just so others won't see you as a person in love with his or her own voice, but while listening to their arguments (whether honest questions or just smoke screens), you are learning who they are and how they think.

You can learn to draw people out so they tell you about themselves. But this takes time and must be done gradually, over a period of time. Will you invest enough time in others to discover who they are and how best to communicate God's love to them? I hope so.

A monologue is merely "semi-communication" or "pseudo-communication." Taylor summarizes this cogently:

> If we want the right to tell our story, however, we must be willing, even eager, to hear the stories of others. And we should listen compassionately, with a bias toward finding common ground rather than listening for an opportunity to attack. This common ground is not the flaccid "everybody is right" of flabby relativism. The goal is not niceness, or pseudo-unanimity, but a core package of values and rights we can affirm together while we continue to

---

[73] McCallum, *The Death of Truth.* p.240.

> disagree on some fundamental understandings of the ultimate nature of things.[74]

The better you listen to what others say, the better you will understand yourself too.

Somehow Christians must learn the art of conversation. Ronald Johnson offers eight tips for engaging a lost person in conversation in order to offer a "redemptive word":

- Tip No. 1: Communicate genuine interest
- Tip No. 2: Comment on the person's life story
- Tip No. 3: Explore a religious concept together
- Tip No. 4: Reinforce your visit
- Tip No. 5: Keep it simple
- Tip No. 6: Test the person's readiness to go further
- Tip No. 7: Recognize those who are ready
- Tip No. 8: Listen[75]

If the meaning of these tips is not clear, you might find a copy of this book in a library and read his explanation for each one.

Spiritual conversations

Some people use the word *conversation* instead of *dialogue*. Hybels and Mittelberg discuss ways to guide conversations to spiritual matters. They suggest creating transitions from everyday concerns to eternal topics.

> The indirect method takes some element of the topic and utilizes it to turn the conversation toward matters of God, the church, or faith. There's almost no limit to the ways this can be done. With a little planning and practice, almost anyone can master this approach.[76]

They continue by offering illustrations of transitions from conversations of business, relocation, hobbies, nature, music, sports, problems, and holidays to discussions of our faith in Christ Jesus.

---

[74] Taylor, "Are You Tolerant?" *Christianity Today*. January 11, 1999, p.52. He uses *pseudo-unanimity* to mean "falsely unanimous."

[75] Ronald Johnson, *How Will They Hear If We Don't Listen?* Broadman & Holman Publishers, 1994, pp.162-168.

[76] Bill Hybels and Mark Mittelberg, *Becoming a Contagious Christian.* Zondervan, 1994, p.141.

Convincing, persuading, & arguing

Most people seem to use the words convince and persuade synonymously, but in years gone by, these two terms had a slightly different meaning. Convince meant to cause someone to believe something is true; persuade meant to cause someone to adopt a certain behavior. Why is this relevant? Our goal is to convince people of the truth of the Gospel, not merely persuade them to adopt a certain lifestyle.

If you present a postmodernist with the truth claims of the Gospel, you had better be prepared for some argument. And *argument* is neither bad nor without precedent.

> *These men began to argue with Stephen, but they could not stand up against his wisdom or the Spirit by whom he spoke. (Acts 6:9-10)*

> *Since, then, we know what it is to fear the Lord, we try to persuade men. (2 Corinthians 5:11)*

Luke ends his book of Acts with a description of how Paul, toward the end of his life, tried to convince people that Jesus is the Savior.

> *They arranged to meet Paul on a certain day, and came in even larger numbers to the place where he was staying. From morning till evening he explained and declared to them the kingdom of God and tried to convince them about Jesus from the Law of Moses and from the Prophets. (Acts 28:23)*

We often use the words *argue* and *argument* as PEJORATIVES, but these words have a good sense too. Don't misunderstand me. We must not be quarrelsome. We certainly don't want to be guilty of thinking of what we will say next, instead of listening to the arguments of the other person. However, we must be able to explain *why* we believe what we believe if we ever hope to convince anyone to place his or her faith in the Lord. Further, we must try to answer the questions that people are asking. And this may sound like an *argument* (in the negative sense).

We must learn how to argue logically and effectively—and calmly—so God can use us to convince people of the truth of the gospel message. But this is only one part of a larger strategy.

Pressing for a decision

Just as a person is not a salesman until someone buys, "teachers teach only when students learn." That was the old proverb I was taught in my college secondary education courses. The salesman presses for the customer to sign on the line, and teachers test to see if students have learned. Is it equally true that we are not witnesses until we "lead someone to Christ"?

✐ Wait a minute! Please don't continue reading. Try to answer the question before you continue.

On one hand, as fishers of men, we are not just trying to influence fish.[77] We want to "catch" them. But there is much more to consider here. We must not be manipulative or so assertive that we usurp God's role, and *we* make converts. The Bible clearly reveals that *God* convicts people of sin, *God's Spirit* draws people to himself, *he* convinces people of the person and work of the Savior, and *he* alone saves. Not us.

One very useful analogy I've heard to describe our role in the salvation of others is that of a midwife. We are just assistants. So we must learn to discern where a person is in the process. Has gestation just begun? Or is rebirth imminent? This comes with practice, with listening, and with being sensitive to the person and the Holy Spirit.

We must not become obsessed with "counting scalps." Measure the success of witnessing in terms of your faithfulness, not in terms of observable results. We may play a different role in the process of several different people coming to Christ. Paul explained the different roles he and Apollos played:

✐ *What, after all, is Apollos? And what is Paul? Only servants, through whom you came to believe—as the Lord has assigned to each his task. I planted the seed, Apollos watered it, but God made it grow. So neither he who plants nor he who waters is anything, but only God, who makes things grow. The man who plants and the man who waters have one purpose, and each will be rewarded according to his own labor. For we are God's fellow workers; you are God's field, God's building. (1 Corinthians 3:5-9)*

Ah, God assigns us our tasks. In one case you may give a verbal witness. In another you may do a loving deed. In another you may simply pray. Don't keep score! Just try to fulfill the task God assigns to you—case by case.

---

[77] Matthew 4:19 and Mark 1:17 quote Jesus telling the fisherman brothers Peter and Andrew that if they would follow him, he would make them fishers of men.

As we press for a decision, we must not use manipulative methods to persuade people to act like Christians. Instead, we should use a holy lifestyle and valid argumentation to convince non-Christians of their lost condition and God's offer of forgiveness. A person can be *persuaded* but remain *unconvinced.*

Witnessing models

Consider Graeme Codrington's description of five methods (tactics or strategies) of witnessing.[78]

- 1. Lifestyle/Relationship/Friendship Evangelism
- 2. Small Group Evangelism
- 3. Social Welfare/Ministry/Service Evangelism
- 4. Corporate Evangelism
- 5. Socratic Evangelism[79]

Codrington argues that though all of these should be linked to the local church, they need not all be centered on the local church. A healthy church body should be using all of these. The primary focus of this book is personal witnessing (model 1 above), but first let's consider how churches can build relationships in order to witness.

Corporate outreach

In the 1950s and 1960s, churches would typically have one or two revivals a year. These would last a week or two, and the church could be assured of adding several new converts. In most parts of our country, this is no longer the case. Today a "great revival" often only

---

[78] Graeme Codrington, "Generation X Papers: Methods of Evangelistic Contact." www.youth.co.za/papers/yevangel.htm.

[79] Probably you are familiar with all of these except the last one. Codrington describes it like this: "The Socratic method is named after the Socrates, the great Greek philosopher, who taught his students by using a method of inductive question and answer. Socrates would guide the student to discover the truth for himself by asking leading questions, and questioning inconsistencies within the student's comments. This method requires discussion and openness, and does not arrogantly tear down other belief-systems, but rather points someone towards the truth. If we believe that the Bible is Truth, then we should have nothing to fear from a proper investigation of the truth - we should believe that it will ultimately lead *to* the God of the Bible." (Codrington, "Generation X Papers: Methods of Evangelistic Contact." home.pix.za/gc/gc12/papers/p1002.htm.)

moves church folks from one church to another—very few unchurched people come to trust in Christ for the first time at a revival. Is a series of evening preaching services in a church building still the best way to win the lost in your hometown?

The leaders of many churches have long recognized the need for new strategies for reaching postmodernists. Typically they look for a need to fill in order to establish a non-spiritual relationship with people. Then, after they have won some level of confidence, they are better able to communicate the Gospel in a meaningful way. Often this comes during a time of transition or during a personal or family crisis.

Let me offer some specific examples. One church offered free computer classes to parents. "Come to church on Monday night," they said, "and we will teach you what your children already know about computers and the Internet." Another church offered free parenting classes to young married couples. They brought in health professionals to tell which immunization shots babies should have and other medical tips for raising healthy children. Of course, later, some of these people said, "Why don't we visit this church one Sunday morning?"

A relationship had been built, a relationship of trust. And that provided the basis for proclaiming the Gospel. Can you think of a better foundation? You see, one-on-one witnessing is not the only kind that requires building a foundation of relationship and trust—corporate witnessing does too.

Only the leading of the Holy Spirit and the creativity of the church leadership limit the possibilities.

> 🖉 List things like this that you've seen churches do to acquaint the community with the local church (like offering a sports clinic).

A friend who pastors a local church told me of how they are reaching out with a community-wide picnic. During the summer they are inviting area residents to come to a park for an afternoon of family games and free food. The free barbecue and soft drinks will attract people and acquaint them with the church. The hope is that some of the church members will begin developing a friendship with some of the guests. Other guests may decide to visit the church.

I know a few young Christian men in San Francisco who love to play salsa music. But when they played in their church, some of the older members objected to this secular music in the church. When I asked José how he responded to the pastor when he told him of this, he said it was no problem. Instead these musicians took their music to Golden Gate Park on the weekends and summer evenings and played their salsa music there. In a few minutes a crowd would gather around them. One or another of them would interject a brief testimony of how God saved him, and then they would play one gospel song and take a break. Invariably, José told me, someone would come up during the break and talk with them about some life problem. Of course, one of the Christians would tell him of his need for the Savior, and sometimes lead him to the Lord. Perhaps the older saints didn't care for salsa music in the church, but God had a use for it in the park!

> ✎ Can you think of other similar things that churches could do to establish relationships with people in the community? Jot them down.

Other people have reached out to people in their neighborhood by inviting them to a Bible study in their homes. They handed out flyers stating the time and day that they would meet and other details. The meeting was very structured so that it did not last too long and people knew that they were committing themselves to a certain number of weeks. Typically they choose one of the Gospels to read through with group discussion.

If you attempt this, you should be prepared for the presence of a cult member. This may mean finding an outside resource person (like a pastor or more mature Christian leader) to attend your meetings. It may also mean laying down some ground rules that might include simply discussing what the text says and applying it to the lives of those present without using commentaries or other books as aids.

Dennis McCallum and a ministry team of Xenos Christian Fellowship have an outreach they call "Conversation and Cuisine."[80] He calls this meal shared by Christians and non-Christians a "pre-evangelistic" event. Its purpose is to expose adults who might be too

---

[80] McCallum, "Conversation and Cuisine." July 6, 1995. www.xenos.org/ministries/justforfun/cc1.htm.

timid to attend a Seekers Meeting to Christians and to home-based fellowship.

Corporate evangelism is treated briefly because it's not the focus of this book. Training individual Christians to witness is one of the best things a church can do to evangelize today—probably better than any other approach.

Reaching an individual

In the Appendix you will find a true story of the struggle I had witnessing to one of my best friends when I'd just become a Christian. It illustrates several things about witnessing. Turn to page 166 in the Appendix and read "A Blessed Depression" now, and then consider the problems you have had witnessing to particular friends or family members.

> ✎ Make notes of what you think this story illustrates and the problems that you have struggled with as you have witnessed.

In order to earn the right to share a witness with a person, you must first establish a relationship of trust. This takes an investment of time and energy. We are so used to living in an "instant" world that many Christians are not willing to invest this amount of time and energy in a relationship with a non-Christian.

James Emery White says it so well in a section titled "Relationships Must Be Built With Nonbelievers" in his essay "Evangelism in a Postmodern World," that I include it here in its entirety for you.

> 📖 The average nonbeliever is functionally insulated from the most common evangelistic approaches. As we noted above, they do not attend revivals. They are not appreciative of door-to-door visits. They do not see a "Jesus Loves You" bumper sticker and feel like pulling off to the side of the road and repenting.
>
> 📖 They will be reached as believers intentionally build relationships with them and share a credible verbal witness. This is the most effective and impactive form of evangelism. It is as simple and profound as that.
>
> 📖 The dilemma today is that few believers have active, healthy relationships with nonbelievers. The typical Christian cannot name three non-Christians they've shared a meal with in the last six months. We have withdrawn into holy huddles and Christian

> cliques. At times, in our politically and socially polarized environment, non-Christians are even viewed as the enemy.
>
> 📖 But they are not the enemy, and the most effective means of evangelism is within the context of a personal relationship where the right to be heard has been won. Nothing is as powerful as a personal testimony and the visible difference of Jesus Christ in a life. In the postmodern world, we must recapture the idea that the kingdom of God is extended one person at a time.[81]

White is profoundly correct as far as describing the social life of most Christians! Are you willing to continue investing time and energy in a friendship, even if after years you do not see that person getting closer to receiving Christ Jesus as Lord and Savior? How long is long enough?

✎ What do you think? You walk into a restaurant and see the Christian couple whose faith-walk you respect most. They don't see you. You notice that they have another couple at their table, and the other couple is drinking beer and smoking cigarettes. You're close enough to overhear some of the conversation, and that other couple uses vulgar and obscene language. What do you think? What do you say the next day to your Christian friends?

✎ Another scenario: You enter a restaurant and see a Christian couple you know at one table and a non-Christian couple you know at another table (and they are smoking and drinking). Both invite you to join them. Which invitation do you accept? Why?

Many Christians today are unwilling to be a close friend with a non-Christian. Possibly they fear it will hurt their image in the Christian community. God help us to recognize that we must be friends with the lost to win them to Christ. How we can effectively accomplish this is a major goal of this book and is developed in later chapters.

And if you find yourself unable to start witnessing to unchurched people, then find some of the unsaved people that you go to church with and try to lead them to the Lord.

Friendship must be sincere and not just for the sake of witnessing. People will spot insincerity, and your insincerity will push them even further from the Lord. Faking a friendship in order to witness to

---

[81] White, "Evangelism in a Postmodern World," pp.367-368.

someone is probably worse than not even trying to witness to them at all.

> ✏ Perhaps the most important thing you can tell a non-Christian is how you became a Christian. Imagine an old friend comes to you because he or she knows you are a Christian and says, "Tell me how I can become a Christian like you." Exactly what would you tell him or her?

Tell me the story of Jesus

As we attempt to tell people of the Savior within the context of the Bible's Big Picture, we must be careful how we relate the Bible stories. Too often people will tell the story of David and Goliath in such a way as to make David the hero or the story of Daniel in the lion's den and make Daniel the hero.

These Bible stories were written first and foremost to reveal things about who God is and what he is doing. He is the hero of all Bible stories. This emphasis is not to ignore humans, just to place us in our proper position.

> ✏ Rethink many of the Old and New Testament stories from this perspective of God as the primary focus and see how it changes what you gain from that story. For instance, what can we learn about God from the account of Gideon? Take notes!

This is true for Bible stories, but it is equally true and important in our relating our own salvation story. Who is the hero of your personal testimony?

Since postmodernists listen to stories, we should use stories to introduce and illustrate biblical truths. But the Bible must control our illustrative stories, and not vice versa.

Perhaps the most powerful story you have to tell any non-Christian is your own testimony of how you became a Christian. You should practice telling this so that you can tell it accurately and succinctly. Like anything else, witnessing improves with practice.

> ✏ One of the best ways to do this is to write it down. Read it aloud to a friend and listen to his or her suggestions for improvement. But do not embellish it! God is not glorified by our exaggerations (lies)! (Consider Romans 6:1-2.)

Your personal story of salvation should clearly illustrate the "Big Picture" of the Bible. How would you describe the Bible's Big Picture? Is it relevant to people of every culture on the earth? How could your testimony be told to better illustrate the Big Picture of God's revelation?

An example of a personal testimony is included in the Appendix. Pause now, bookmark this page, and go read "God's Amazing Grace: A Personal Testimony" on page 170.

> ✐ Make notes of what you see as the strengths and weaknesses of this account of my personal testimony in witnessing to a postmodernist.

Indispensable follow-up

I cannot overemphasize the importance of follow-up. We must not act as midwives, assisting in a person's rebirth experience, if we are unwilling to invest the time and energy to help new converts grow to a level of maturity where they can feed and care for themselves. An important part of this follow-up is fellowship—relationships with other Christians.

We must enroll them in a local church. We must teach them the importance of the spiritual disciplines like Bible study, prayer, corporate fellowship, and worship. And this will take time and energy too. But we must also help them develop and maintain safe relationships with non-Christians, as you will see in a later chapter.

In what ways are you willing to be available to people to whom you witness? In what ways are you *not* willing to be available to people to whom you witness? You should settle this before you get involved with people.

What about follow-up to people to whom you have witnessed, but they have yet to receive Christ? Should you have a follow-up strategy for these, too?

My personal conviction is that witnessing and follow-up should be connected to a local church. You should have all of this in mind before you start trying to lead someone to the Lord.

> ✐ Why should witnessing be connected to a local church? What is the advantage of the local church in witnessing? What is the disadvantage in not being connected to a local church?

Finally, we spoke in an earlier chapter of tools that we have for witnessing. Whatever strategies we try to develop for witnessing, they should include using the tools we have at our disposal.

A postmodern strategy

Christians must use our knowledge of postmodernism to develop witnessing strategies that fit our audience. Here's how one writer describes it:

> 📖 The overall need is for evangelism that demonstrates partnership, co-operation across boundaries, and an integrated approach that acknowledges truth beyond our own minds. Evangelism should follow Christ's example and make more use of stories (or micronarratives) and be careful not to use brittle metanarratives as control tools. It should reach all corners of society. Mystery may seem in conflict with evangelism but actually it can diminish the pull to dance for the rational mind. Logic is not the only way to present Christ and draw a response of faith and repentance. Evangelism should also recognise God's plan to renew the whole of creation and avoid preaching a human-centred gospel. Reality as a focus of postmodernity leads evangelism to offer genuine spiritual experience through Christ. It may also create opportunities to present him as real hope and truth in the midst of a postmodern mosaic of stories and ideas.[82]

Without a doubt, we will have to use everything God gives us to accomplish this task: our minds, our talents, and the gifts of the Holy Spirit! And this will require self-discipline and hard work.

Witnessing that is most effective to a postmodern usually uses the common language of the audience (rather than church jargon), uses stories (especially your own testimony and Bible stories), includes conversational dialogue, and often uses analogies.

French mathematician and philosopher Blaise Pascal said, "There is a God-shaped hole in every heart." People attempt to fill that void a variety of ways, but only God will satisfy. We need to help people discover that hole and show them that the Savior—and nothing else—fills it perfectly.

---

[82] Anonymous, "Christian Tradition, Post-modern Worldview and Evangelism." www.churcharmy.com.au/E3.htm.

So do not be ashamed to testify about our Lord...
2 Timothy 1:8

Chapter 9
No Pain, No Gain

Grow and witness

If you reflect on your Christian life and conclude that you have not been a good witness, don't despair. We Christians were not reborn fully grown. Peter told his readers to "grow in the grace and knowledge of our Lord and Savior Jesus Christ." (2 Peter 3:18) And that exhortation to keep on growing serves us well today too.

Maturation is a process. Peter had already addressed it earlier:

🕊 *For this very reason, make every effort to add to your faith goodness; and to goodness, knowledge; and to knowledge, self-control; and to self-control, perseverance; and to perseverance, godliness; and to godliness, brotherly kindness; and to brotherly kindness, love. For if you possess these qualities in increasing measure, they will keep you from being ineffective and unproductive in your knowledge of our Lord Jesus Christ. (2 Peter 1:5-8)*

You will have to make an effort to grow in Christlikeness and avoid becoming an ineffective, unproductive Christian.

A big part of maturation consists of identifying and rejecting the false aspects of our culture that helped to shape our worldview. We must also work to discover what (biblical) truth is absent from our worldview (because of the influence of our culture), and embrace those truths. And this takes time and requires work—it sure has for me.

Just as our spiritual growth is a never-ending process, our learning to witness will always be a work in progress. The methods you learn today may not work when you are my age, because our culture will likely keep changing. Jim Leffel warns us that:

📖 The task of apologetics is ongoing because cultural ideas, concerns, and attitudes change rapidly. Consequently, there will never be a "definitive" work on apologetics. Indeed, when we think such a work exists we are in trouble. Apologetics is an ongoing work, needing constant revision as new ideological elements enter into social discourse.[83]

If you hope to be an effective Christian, you'll have to be a learner all of your life, not just while you're in high school or college! Isn't that encouraging? Your involvement in a local church should meet this need.

To grow physically, you need to breathe air, drink liquids, eat a well-balanced diet, exercise, and get plenty of sleep. But how do you grow spiritually? Several years ago I wrote a piece that addressed this very question. "Seven Habits of Highly Effective Christians" is reprinted below. Please read and reflect on it now.

&ᘐᘐᘐᘐᘐᘐᘐᘐᘐᘐᘐᘐᘐᘐᘐᘐᘐᘐᘐᘐᘐᘐᘐᘐᘐᘐᘐᘐᘐᘐᘐᘐᘐ&

Seven Habits of Highly Effective Christians
By Steve Badger
[First published in *The Pentecostal Evangel*, Jan. 9, 1994.]

1. Highly Effective Christians habitually spend "quality time" with God (alone in Bible study and reflection, two-way prayer, and meditation, and corporately in worship) empowering them to live a life of faith. (Psalm 1; Ps 91)

2. Highly Effective Christians habitually work at developing personal relationships with both Christians and non-Christians (handling conflicts & solving problems), because they realize that love and forgiveness are what you do and not just what you feel or say. (1 Corinthians 13:13; 1 John 1:7-11; 3:16-18)

3. Highly Effective Christians habitually manage their time, invest their money, and structure their values according to Kingdom principles instead of the World's. (Matthew 5-7)

4. Highly Effective Christians habitually seek to be refilled with the Holy Spirit, allowing Him to always produce His fruit and manifest His gifts. (Galatians 5:22; Ephesians 5:18)

---

[83] Leffel, "The New Challenge in Christian Apologetics." Presentation to Cornell University Faculty, April 1999, www.crossrds.org/cornell.htm.

5. Highly Effective Christians habitually look at problems and blessings from an eternal (vs. temporal) and spiritual (vs. human) perspective. (1 Corinthians 2:14)
6. Highly Effective Christians have developed the habit of periodically re-prioritizing and re-ordering their lives so that they follow and obey the Good Shepherd. (Psalms 23; Matthew 6:33; John 10:3-5,27; 2 Corinthians 13:5-6)
7. Highly Effective Christians are habitually faithful to their commitments—to the Lord, to the Church, to family and friends, to employers and/or employees—regardless of the personal cost. (1 Corinthians 10:31; Hebrews 10:25; Revelation 2:10-11)

You cannot become a Christian by developing these habits. But Christians who possess these habits are effective in affecting the world for Christ Jesus.

> ✐ Interesting, isn't it, that I did not include witnessing in that list. Would you want it included? What else is not there that you think should be included? What is there that you think should be omitted? You might forget...so write it in your journal.

We need to see our sanctification as both an event and a process. The transformation that God's Spirit makes in the life of the believer is past, present, and future. And this process will not be completed this side of eternity—no matter how long you live or how mature you become.

Paul told the Christians in Corinth that he was waging a war.

🕊 *For though we live in the world, we do not wage war as the world does. The weapons we fight with are not the weapons of the world. On the contrary, they have divine power to demolish strongholds. We demolish arguments and every pretension that sets itself up against the knowledge of God, and we take captive every thought to make it obedient to Christ. (2 Corinthians 10:3-5)*

How do you suppose Paul was able to demolish arguments? Is it unreasonable to respond that Paul had a better, stronger, more rational argument? How will you demolish the postmodern pretensions that set themselves up against the knowledge of God today? It's not only your own thoughts you need to take captive! The fallacious thoughts of those who are enemies of the Cross of Christ Jesus need to be refuted with the truth of the Gospel. If we don't do it, who will?

I join those who are praying that God will raise up an army of Christians who are willing to pay the price in time and effort to excel academically and prepare themselves for this warfare. Have you enlisted? Are you in boot camp? Are you helping to fight the war?

You don't have to be a college student to "excel academically." Find a church with a good training program and get enrolled.

A lost doctrine

A few generations ago people heard a lot at church about a doctrine called stewardship. Most people today are not even familiar with the word *steward*. A steward is a person who is put in charge of the property of another. So stewardship refers to how you manage what has been entrusted to you.

What is it that God has entrusted to you? Christians are accountable to God for what we do with *all* of our abilities, talents, finances, possessions, time, relationships—and everything I've left out.

Do you think that our responsibility to God is met by giving our church a tithe (ten percent) of our income and regularly attending church services? The biblical concept is quite different. We are accountable to God for all that we have, all that we are, and all that we do.

✎ How does stewardship relate to personal witnessing?

What's important to you?

I encourage you to evaluate your life to try to find out what your priorities are. Is this just a little frightening? It probably should be.

One way to gain some insights into your priorities is to tally two things: how you spend your money and how you spend your time. What would you conclude if you spend more money on entertainment than you give to support Kingdom work? What would you think if you discovered that you spent more time watching your favorite TV show than you do reading and reflecting on God's Word? What occupies your thinking?

Be careful now. I spend more money each month on my house than I do for food and nothing at all for air—but food and air are more important. So all I am suggesting is that these two evaluations will help you to discover what your priorities are.

✎ Most people will never evaluate how they spend their money and time. Without getting overly legalistic, keep a time and expenditure log for one week and try to discover your priorities.

Learning by doing

Wayne was a college student studying to be a minister, and he was embarrassed by the fact that he had never witnessed to anyone. One fall he returned to college a changed man. That summer he had gone to work with an evangelist who headed a beach ministry on the Texas gulf coast.

When Wayne first arrived, the evangelist promised all of the students that he would teach them how to witness. For a week they spent all morning reading the Bible, discussing what they read, and praying together. Then the second week he loaded them up, drove to the beach, paired each guy up with a girl, and told them to go witness to people on the beach.

Wayne felt betrayed and became quite angry. This evangelist had not made good on his promise! He had not taught him how to witness. Though discouraged, Wayne went with his teammate on the beach and within just a few minutes she began witnessing to a girl while Wayne watched and listened. As the morning progressed Wayne found himself witnessing to a young man about his own age.

Wayne had not learned how to witness that first week. He learned the second week. He learned by doing. The best way to learn how to witness is by witnessing. You can have this same experience.

But you won't have this experience if you just stay in the classroom studying witnessing. You'll have to leave your church or school, build a relationship with a non-Christian, develop a strategy based on what you learn about this person, open your mouth, and share your rebirth experience and faith with him or her. And then you'll have to live faithfully for the King.

103

And if you cannot do that as a student (or wherever you are in life today), what makes you think you could do that as a pastor, or a youth pastor, or a missionary—or even as a Christian lay person?

The words of that old chorus come to mind repeatedly:

Lord, lay some soul upon my heart, and love that soul through me.
And may I ever do my part to win that soul for Thee.

A lost spiritual discipline

One of the most important spiritual disciplines is very often overlooked if not rejected by many Christians. Every Christian needs to be involved in some kind of a program of study, of learning—though not necessarily in a classroom setting. The object of our study needs to be the Bible and how what it says applies to our lives. This is not intended to limit our study to the Bible itself; God has used many gifted scholars, teachers, and preachers to write both devotional and technical books that can help us to understand what the Bible says.

Bible study is a waste of time—until and unless we allow the Holy Spirit to apply it to our lives and change us into the image of the Savior.

Through the years the church has attempted to meet this need with a variety of programs, the most widely known is usually called Sunday school. Many churches have also held a mid-week Bible study (which in many churches is not Bible study but something else). Small groups (cell groups) meeting in homes are also an effective vehicle for Bible study.

Far too few Christians are willing to discipline themselves to study what God says in his Word. But there is just no substitute for personal Bible study.

What do we gain from personal Bible study? Consider these:
- The Christian interacts with God during Bible study.
- We discover more about God's nature and personality.
- We become aware of God's purposes in creation.
- We learn to worship him in spirit and in truth.
- We discover how God has acted in human history, and thus how God will act today.
- We learn more about ourselves and human nature and God's purposes in creating us.

- We realize the on-going struggle we all have with the world, the flesh, and the devil.
- We gain a more objective perspective of right and wrong.

The Bible is not our only object of study. We must also study (1) the non-Christians we hope to win and (2) effective communication skills. But it is in personal Bible study that the Christian meets and interacts with the Spirit of Christ Jesus—and he transforms us into his image, producing his character traits in us. And this is essential to becoming an effective witness.

*It was he who gave some to be...evangelists...so
that the body of Christ may be built up.*
Ephesians 4:11-12

Chapter 10
Three Encounters of the Close Kind

Is this the only way?

The strategy of building a network of relationships for the purpose of witnessing is so emphasized in this book, that I feel compelled to balance it with a restatement of the truth that God does at times use strangers to lead the lost to himself. I also want to reaffirm the biblical function of the evangelist. In Ephesians 4:11-13, Paul tells us that God provides the church with apostles, evangelists, pastors, and teachers to build his Body.

Notice in verse 12 that Paul tells us that the God gives the Body these leaders "to prepare God's people for works of service." And I am convinced these "works of service" include witnessing. The task is too big to be accomplished by professional ministers alone—every Christian must get involved in winning the lost!

Consider Philip and the Ethiopian eunuch in Acts 8:26-40. They had no prior relationship. But the Holy Spirit led them together and used Philip to lead him to faith. I do not want to minimize the function of the evangelist. I only want to recognize that God has *not* called all of us to be evangelists, *but* he has called all Christians to witness to what he has done in our lives.

Please don't read the following true accounts of my experiences and jump to the conclusion that God wants you to pick up hitchhikers and witness to them. He may, or he may not. Picking up hitchhikers can be extremely dangerous, and Christians have responsibilities to their families too. On the other hand, if you see someone hitchhiking, and you are absolutely certain that God wants you to give him a ride and tell him of his great love, remember, the consequences just may be eternal![84]

---

[84] Let me emphasize that you should not imagine that my experiences are authoritative—I certainly do not think that. Our authority in faith and practice is

Jesse (Summer, 1972, Mississippi)

Mississippi had a bad race-relations reputation, and this south Mississippi town's was as bad as any. A few years before I had this experience, a young African-American man had been lynched, and no one had been punished for it. I had just shared a Pentecostal testimony in a local Baptist church and was driving home in the summer darkness discussing the experience with my wife, when I saw him.

Actually he wasn't hitchhiking, just hiking northward on the interstate shoulder. Since it was a hot summer night I stopped to offer him a lift. Until he came up to my van I did not know he was African-American.

"Hi, d'you want a ride?" I shouted to him. He paused as he considered my offer. "I'll be happy to let you ride with us," I continued. With much reluctance, he climbed into my van. "My name's Steve," I said as I offered him my hand.

"I'm Jesse," he responded quietly and gave me a handshake. He was a slender man and looked to be in his mid-forties.

Jesse got the unabridged version of my testimony on the hour-long journey toward my home—the usual price required of all hitchhikers who accepted my offer of a ride. He listened as well as most, but showed no response.

He told us that he was heading home to his wife and children in Alabama. He said that he'd gone to New Orleans to bail his brother out of jail, but he had been mugged, beaten, and robbed of the bail money.

As we neared town, Jesse finally responded to my witnessing, "That's all real nice, but do you know where I can get something to eat? I haven't eaten in two days."

I couldn't wait to tell him. "I sure do! I know where to get the best food anywhere in this town." Of course, we took him to our house. While Jesse was eating, we saw the welts on his arms from mosquito bites and offered him some relief.

After he had a hot bath and put lotion on his bites, we sat in the living room, and I continued witnessing to him. During the hour or so that we talked, I sensed that he was so grateful for our help that he

---

the Bible alone. But sometimes our experiences illustrate biblical truths—and I hope these do.

would do almost anything to please us. But I didn't want him to kneel and repeat a prayer that would not result in the miraculously-changed life that only God could give, so I asked him to promise me that he would read the modern English translation of the New Testament that I had given him and seek God's salvation through Jesus. He promised he would try. My wife and I went to our bedroom while he bedded down on the couch in the living room.

The next day a church donated the money to buy Jesse a bus ticket home to his family in Alabama. I never heard from him again, and do not know if he ever received the Lord. But I think of Jesse from time to time.

> ✐ What do you think I could have done better in witnessing to Jesse? Should I have pressed Jesse to kneel and pray "the sinner's prayer" with me?

Jeff (March, 1976, Texas)

I was on the wrong road. I don't know how long I had been on it, but it was definitely the wrong road. Not that it wouldn't take me back to Lake Jackson, Texas—it would—but I had decided to avoid the delay of the small towns by taking another route instead. A Christian friend, Jack, had let me use his car to go to Corpus Christi, and I was on my way back to his house between Houston and Galveston.

Forget it, I thought to myself, it would take longer to go back and pick up the right road than to continue. Besides, maybe God has some purpose for this mistake.

I had been trusting Jesus for about five years, had experienced the Baptism in the Holy Spirit, and had seen God do many amazing things, but I was about to get another installment in a series of lessons on obedience.

The hitchhiker was a tall blonde with a beautiful ponytail and a tan seen only in Coppertone advertisements. He stood with his duffel bag and surfboard, arm and thumb outstretched. I had often picked up hitchhikers to share my faith in Jesus with them, but for some reason unknown to me, I had no intention of stopping for this long-haired surf-bum.

Then God's Spirit spoke within me instructing me to pick him up. I disobeyed. I drove on. I wrestled with God for the next several minutes, driving further from him.

"God," I argued silently, "it isn't my car, it's Jack's. What if something happens to it?"

Even as I thought that, I could hears Jack's voice in my mind. As I was thanking him profusely for letting me borrow his car, he replied, "It ain't my car, man, it's Jesus'." Though filled with wrong attitudes, I finally said, "OK, God, I'll go back and get him, but he's probably gone by now."

When I saw him, I thought I would drive past him, out of sight, then turn around and come back. I didn't want him thinking I was a homosexual trying to make a pickup. "No," I thought, still annoyed with God for making me come back, "I'll let him see me turn around, then I bet he won't want to ride with me."

I was wrong. He eagerly accepted my offer of a ride and, with a surfboard lengthwise between us, Jeff and I started to get to know each other. He told me how he bummed back-and-forth between his divorced parents' residences. Finally I asked him the question I had asked so many others. "Jeff, has anyone ever told you about Jesus?"

I honestly don't remember his reply, but he and I talked about the Lord for the next couple of hours. Many times he cried, at first with restraint, then freely. Jeff did not receive Jesus' offer of forgiveness then, but he did ask me to drive him to his home and tell his mother about Jesus.

Jeff's mother was cordial, but she was late for work. After listening to a few minutes of my witness, she left. Later, as I left, I invited Jeff to continue with me to Lake Jackson and Jack's house, and I was a little surprised when he accepted my offer.

Jack and his wife were both warm and friendly and shared with Jeff how they had come to trust Jesus. After supper, Jack invited us to go to a prayer meeting where he was to lead the singing. Surely, I thought, Jeff will pray to receive the Lord here. He seemed so receptive to the Gospel.

The meeting came to a close without Jeff even showing an interest in God's salvation. So Jack finally asked him! "Jeff, would you like to pray right now to receive eternal life?"

"Yes, I would," came his answer—and he did!

A few months later we received letters from Jeff telling how his whole family had received Jesus, and they were worshipping in a full-gospel church and growing in faith. I kept his letters.

Wouldn't you think that having had such an experience, I would remember this lesson for a long time? Alas, I didn't learn my lessons well.

Steve (June/July, 1976, Illinois)

It was only three months later—four at the most. I was living near Peoria, Illinois, for the summer with my wife and three children while I was doing biochemical research in a government research laboratory. I had a thirty-minute ride to and from work. After a racquetball game and a good hot shower at the YMCA, I was on my way home—late and hurrying so that my wife wouldn't worry about me.

The highway lay in front of me almost perfectly due east. A solid wall of black clouds went from the north to the south in front of me—I was headed into a violent summer thunderstorm. Then I saw him: a hippie hitchhiker who looked like he was long overdue for a good hot bath.

God's Spirit spoke to me as plainly as I have ever heard Him speak, "Stop. Give him a ride. Tell him." Surely anyone who had experienced the lessons I had recently would obey. No. I drove right past him.

Why? Well look at my situation.

I was headed into the worst storm I had seen all summer. There was no way I could witness to him for ten or twelve miles and then drop him off in this weather beside the road.

On the other hand, I didn't want to take him home with me. "Home" was a camping trailer with my wife, three children, and a dog. Just not enough room. And how would my wife react to this hippie-looking kid spending the night with us? No, I couldn't pick him up, so I drove on past.

As I drove by, he did a real jig on the edge of the highway trying to persuade me to stop, and as I drove on the Spirit spoke these words in my mind, "Inasmuch as you fail to do this to the least of these…" Was He telling me that I had refused to stop and pick up Jesus? "God, forgive me!" I whispered, but no forgiveness came.

"Repent," His Spirit whispered.

"Oh, yes, I repent." Tears literally squirted out of my eyes onto the inside of my glasses.

"No. Repent. Turn around. Turn around, go back and get him." By God's grace I obeyed.

There was another exit just a mile past the exit where he had been dancing, so in just a couple of minutes I had returned and stopped to pick him up. He got in the car just before the rainfall escalated to maximum downpour.

"Hi. I'm Steve," I said.

"Far out man, my name's Steve, too," he replied as he took my outstretched hand.

"Did you notice that I passed you by and then came back to get you?"

"I thought that was you. Thanks for coming back and picking me up."

"Don't thank me. I passed you by. My Boss made me come back and get you." He checked out the empty back seat for my Boss as I continued. "About five years ago I found Jesus as my Savior and Boss. Jesus literally lives inside me now."

"Oh yeah," he said, "We all have some of Jesus inside of us."

"I don't know who told you that, but it's not true. The Bible says only those who become His children have His Spirit living inside them."

This started a full and free discussion that continued all the way home in the driving rain. Just before we arrived he told me, "God has been drawing me for a year."

"Where did you learn that phrase?" I asked. "Where did you hear the phrase 'God drawing'?"

"Nowhere. It's just what I've been feeling, that's all."

I told him that the Bible said God had to draw a man in order for him to come to God. I was excited. Steve would surely get saved tonight!

My whole family did a wonderful job of making Steve feel welcome. He ate and then showered. We talked until bedtime, but he did not pray for salvation.

I was a little disappointed as we all lay in the dark in that one-room trailer. As a final thought I asked him, "Steve, have you ever

111

received something that you knew was a gift only from God?" He said he wasn't sure but indicated I should continue.

"Well, I want to make sure you understand that the food you ate and this dry, clean, warm bed is not compliments of me. I passed you by. I decided to leave you on the highway. Jesus insisted I pick you up. Don't thank me. Thank Him. It is a gift only from Him." And with that we went to sleep.

Next morning on my way to work I gave him a ride to the highway for him to continue his hitchhiking journey. I gave him a modern English New Testament with my name and address in the front. "If you find Jesus, I sure would like to know. Would you write and tell me?" He assured me he would and left.

How disappointing. He sure seemed ready to me. He had said that God was drawing him. Maybe I had failed to witness correctly. Maybe I gave up too easily. Maybe, maybe, maybe…

A full year later I was working at another government research lab in another state. Every week or two I would call my office at home and inquire about any mail. On one such call my secretary said I had a letter from Idaho.

"Utah," I corrected her, "it's from Bill in Utah. I don't know anybody in Idaho."

"No. It's Idaho."

"I don't know anyone in Idaho. It's Utah."

"It says Idaho, and I'm sitting here looking at it."

"Well, open it and read it to me," I said.

After a moment she said, "I can't read this. It's too personal."

"Read it," I said.

It took some encouraging, but finally she read,

📖 Dear Steve,

📖 I don't know if you'll remember me, but you picked me up hitchhiking last summer…I want to say thank you…because the seed of our Lord you planted in me grew!

Yes, Steve had temporarily lost my mailing address but—Praise God!—he had come to trust in Jesus! He wrote me to let me know just as soon as he found my address. I received my encouragement a full year later. I still have that letter. I re-read it today.

I learned more than one lesson from my experience with this hitchhiker, lessons it seems I have to learn over and over again. Jesus wants our homes—no matter how humble or great they are— sacrificed to his rule. This was also one of many times God illustrated that my task is sowing the seed, producing the harvest is his task.

Jesse, Jeff, and Steve are only three of many that God has used to teach me how to serve and obey him.

> ✎ What do these three accounts illustrate? What have you gained from them?

So what?

So thank God for the people who can lead strangers to Christ, but don't feel guilty if you cannot. Be faithful in doing what you know God wants you to do. Pray for those who are gifted in ways you are not.

> ✤ *Now you are the body of Christ, and each one of you is a part of it. (1 Corinthians 12:27)*

> ✎ Do you know anyone brought to Christ by a stranger? Has God ever used you to bring a stranger to repentance and salvation? Have you ever felt guilty because you are unable to witness to strangers?

Every Christian is not an evangelist or a missionary, but all of us have the responsibility of supporting evangelism and missions with prayer and finances.

Let me repeat some information presented earlier. How can a Christian determine which gifts the Spirit is giving him or her? Two books that have surveys to help you answer this question are Kenneth Cain Kinghorn's *Discovering Your Spiritual Gifts: A Personal Inventory Method* (Francis Asbury Press, 1981), and Tim Blanchard's *A Practical Guide to Finding and Using Your Spiritual Gifts* (Tyndale House, 1983). Over a period of time, however, your spiritual gifts should become apparent both to you and to others. (Others are named in Chapter 5.)

> ✎ How has God's Spirit gifted you? How can you use those gifts, directly or indirectly, to lead non-Christians to faith in Christ?

As iron sharpens iron, so one man sharpens another.
Proverbs 27:17

Chapter 11
Don't Scare the Fish Away!

No excuse for inaction

Though I reject witnessing methods and formulas, I do think there are many witnessing errors we should learn to avoid. But you must not let the risk of making mistakes paralyze you. You will almost certainly make some mistakes. I've made plenty. We all do. This chapter is here so we can learn from each other and minimize our errors. So relax, and just try to learn what you can. And if you make some mistakes not cited here, pass them along to me. I want to learn from you too.

Language matters

Every culture and subculture has words that are considered taboo by most people. We learn which words are taboo from our families first, then our peer groups and institutions, and then from the larger subculture. Using words your hearers consider prohibited in polite company will usually weaken your witness.

On the other hand, using common language is usually helpful in witnessing. More precisely, the words you use should fit the educational level and vocabulary of the person you are witnessing to. Don't talk over her head, but don't talk down to her.

The books of the New Testament were written in a form of Greek called Koiné, which means common. If God used the common Greek (rather than the more formal Classical or Attic Greek) to communicate his truth, we can also use our common language to communicate his invitation of salvation to people.

So use common language people will easily understand, but avoid slang or taboo words that can distract from your witness.

Avoid using "Zion language" in your witnessing. Use good, simple English with those who do not appear to be educated, and use the best English you can without sounding forced to those who are educated. When you must use religious jargon or symbols, be sure to explain them.

> ✎ What do these phrases mean? (1) The blood of Jesus. (2) The cross of Christ. Does Christ's blood save us? What does this mean? Do we need to explain this to non-Christians?

Scripture twisting

Don't quote or paraphrase a Bible text out of context to try to make it say something it does not say. One example is Revelation 3:20.

✞ *"Behold, I stand at the door, and knock: if any man hear my voice, and open the door, I will come in to him, and will sup with him, and he with me." (King James Version)*

I've heard this quoted to unsaved people, telling them that Jesus is saying this to lost people. Open your Bible and read it in context. Christ is saying this to the church at Laodicea, not to the lost! Is it okay to use this text as an invitation to the lost? If you do, you are exalting yourself as the authority instead of the Bible. Is this what you want to do? I hope not. Find another text to quote instead of misapplying this one.

> ✎ Suggest some Bible verses that tell the lost of God's invitation to trust him for salvation. Writing them down in your journal will help you remember them.

God's promises—or yours?

This is often related to the previous error. In witnessing, we must not offer false hope.

Have you ever heard a Christian tell someone that if they believe in Jesus Christ, he will solve all their problems? They say, Unhappy? Become a Christian and Christ will make you happy. Financial problems? Medical problems? Whatever it is that's bothering you? Become a Christian, and God will solve your problem. Does God make these promises? He does not—this is contrary to the Scriptures.

Some well-meaning Christians have told unsaved people (or even new converts) that God has promised us that if we will trust him, he will not only save us, but also our families. Has God promised to save your household?

Those who answer "Yes" often base their answer on Acts 16:31. Paul and Silas were in prison in Philippi, when God used an earthquake to set them free. The jailer awakened, thought the prisoners had escaped, and he was about to commit suicide to prevent a more painful execution (for losing his prisoners). Paul interrupted him. So the jailer asked Paul what he had to do to be saved.

> *They replied, "Believe in the Lord Jesus, and you will be saved—you and your household."*

Now, was Paul saying if the jailer believed, he and his household would be saved? Or that if the jailer believed, he would be saved— and the same was true for his household? If you allow the light of the rest of the New Testament to inform your thinking, you will discover that the latter understanding is preferable to the former.

Exaggerations

Sad to say, many Christians find it easy, when speaking of the Savior, to exaggerate either what he has done for them or how sinful a life they have lived. They just want to make the Lord look good. God does not need our exaggerations in order to make him look good. He is already maximally superlative. Paul wrote,

> *Shall we go on sinning so that grace may increase? By no means! (Romans 6:1-2)*

So tell it just as it happened and trust God to use the unvarnished truth to bring the lost to himself.

> ✏ Earlier you were given the assignment to consider this proverb: "A person with an *experience* is never at the mercy of a person with an *argument*." Is this statement true? Now reconsider it and ask yourself these questions: How would you respond if a Mormon or a member of the Jehovah's Witnesses quoted this proverb to you? How would you change this maxim to make it true?

Using secular materials

Can we use non-biblical materials in our witnessing? I would respond with a qualified "Yes." But we must be sure that we do not afford these non-biblical materials the same authority that we ascribe to the Scriptures. For this we have Scriptural precedent.

In Acts we read that Paul introduced his witness to the Athenian philosophers by pointing to a secular artifact.

> ℘ *Paul then stood up in the meeting of the Areopagus and said: "Men of Athens! I see that in every way you are very religious. For as I walked around and looked carefully at your objects of worship, I even found an altar with this inscription: TO AN UNKNOWN GOD. Now what you worship as something unknown I am going to proclaim to you. (Acts 17:22-23)*

Notice how quickly he left that pagan altar and shifted to the Gospel.

We also have a biblical precedent for using secular materials in Paul's letters (e.g., Titus 1:12). In his argument to the church in Corinth concerning the resurrection, Paul warned his readers:

> ℘ *"Bad company corrupts good character." (1 Corinthians 15:33)*

This was a well-known saying at that time in Corinth. Here Paul was quoting the comedy entitled *Thais* by the Greek poet Menander. I think these New Testament examples caution us against jumping to the wrong conclusion about using secular materials.

Let me offer these modern day scenarios for your consideration. As I am dialoguing with a non-Christian friend, the issue of integrity arises. I know he studied British literature in college. Am I limited to the Scriptures? Or can I appropriately quote this part of Shakespeare's *Hamlet* to make a point?

> 📖 This above all: to thine ownself be true,
> And it must follow, as the night the day,
> Thou canst not then be false to any man.

This same friend and I are discussing marriage and divorce. Am I limited to Bible texts, or can I appropriately quote Shakespeare's Sonnet CXVI?

> 📖 Let me not to the marriage of true minds
> Admit impediments. Love is not love
> Which alters when it alteration finds,
> Or bends with the remover to remove.
> Oh no! It is an ever fixed mark
> That looks on tempests and is never shaken.
> ⋯⋯⋯⋯⋯⋯⋯⋯⋯
> If this be error and upon me proved,
> I never writ, nor no man ever loved.

What if you and your non-Christian friend have read some of the same books or seen some of the same movies? Is it appropriate to use these as a touchstone, as an aid in witnessing? We can use these secular texts to find common ground and build a relationship of trust.

117

Pardon my echo, but it bears repeating: we must not afford these extrabiblical materials the same authority that we afford the Holy Scriptures.

When you do make a mistake

God does not require us to know everything. God does not require us to never make any mistakes. What is required of us, God's stewards?

 🕊 *Now it is required that those who have been given a trust must prove faithful. (1 Corinthians 4:2)*

This is what God requires of us. We are entrusted with the message of salvation, and we must be found faithful. At times God will even use our mistakes. Consider the following personal experiences.

While I was teaching in a state university, I traveled to Cincinnati to learn cell culture techniques in a government research laboratory. My wife and I stayed almost a week in a small privately owned motel.

Almost every day the Holy Spirit prompted me to go and witness to the man who worked behind the front desk. I regret to have to tell you that I disobeyed every time. As we were packing the car to leave, I took a gospel tract and a paperback, modern English translation of the New Testament and left it there for the cleaning lady.

Several days later I received a letter that surprised me. I did not know that the man behind the front desk was the owner of the motel, and he cleaned my room. His letter told me that he found the tract and the New Testament, and as he read the tract, God's Spirit so convicted him that he knelt at the bed and prayed for forgiveness. He had served the Lord years ago, but he was far from Christ at that time.

What a blessing I had missed! I could have been fellowshipping with him all week long, and I could have been building him up in the faith.

A few years later, I was serving in my local church as the director of a mission outreach in a very poor neighborhood of our city. One of our Sunday school teachers told me that one of the youngsters told him that a rat had bitten him. I felt compelled to visit their home and make sure his parents understood the serious nature of this injury.

118

When I arrived at their home, his 70-plus-year-old grandfather was sitting on the porch in a rocking chair. Grandpa told me that no one else was home. As I turned to leave, I felt the nudge of the Holy Spirit to witness to this man. I wish I had a transcript of our conversation—almost everything I said was negative!

I turned and said something like, "I don't suppose you want someone to sit and visit with you." He pointed to the porch swing and invited me to sit down. We made small talk for a few minutes, and then I asked him if anyone had ever told him about Jesus.

"Not really," was his reply.

"Well I don't suppose you'd like me to tell you now," I said.

"Yes, I would," he said. And so I did just that.

As I finished explaining in simple terms the Gospel message, I asked him, "I don't suppose you'd like to pray and confess your sins and ask God to forgive you because of Jesus' death, would you?"

"Yes, I would," he answered.

"But I mean you wouldn't want to pray right here on the porch right now, would you?"

And one last time he said, "Yes, I would." And we did.

Now you can rationalize this with an explanation like, well maybe that low-key witness was the only kind he could receive. And perhaps that's right. But a negative approach is not a typical approach.

So don't let your mistakes or failures quench the Spirit. Learn from them and trust God to cover over your errors. We must never forget McGrath's admonition that our witnessing is "not about winning arguments—it is about winning people." [85]

---

[85] McGrath, *Intellectuals Don't Need God & Other Modern Myths*. p.12.

Crispus...and his entire household
believed in the Lord.
Acts 18:8

Chapter 12
Get Your Fishing Tackle Ready

What happened to me?

Let me repeat that I do not subscribe to any formula or method or gimmick for witnessing. I don't mean to offend anyone by saying that, only to speak the truth—I hope in love. But I do embrace a particular strategy, and I think far too few Christians have any strategy in mind when it comes to witnessing!

When I was in graduate school, I was far from the Lord. Even though I had grown up in a Christian home, even though I had had experiences with Christ, even though I was going to church somewhat regularly, I was living for myself. My father and a Christian friend, Ed, "conspired" behind my back and targeted me for salvation. (This story is in the Appendix on page 170.)

Ed was also in graduate school at the university. He invested time in me, developed a friendship with me. And late one night, when the time was right, he carefully shared the Gospel with me. And that witness bore fruit in my life. For the first time as a "mature, consenting adult," I prayed, confessing my sins and asking Jesus to be my Lord and Savior.

The story is too long to tell here, but—sad to say—I lived for the Lord only a few months and then fell away. By God's grace, I came back to him a few years later. I thank God for his mercy to me.

In late 1971 I was still in graduate school and married with two children when God brought me back to repentance and faith in him. Only one of my close friends was a Christian. All of the rest of my friends were living very sinful lives—just as I had been.

Now I was witnessing to people almost every day. Hardly a week went by that God didn't use me to lead one or two people to salvation, often at the university, but sometimes on the streets.

I would look at the members of my church and wonder if they were really Christians. I never heard of them witnessing. I never heard of them leading anyone to Christ. Could they be genuine Christians? And I prayed that I would never become whatever they were. But over the years, to my private embarrassment, I did just that.

What had happened to me? This shocked me, shamed me, confused me, and depressed me! How could this happen? I prayed about it. I thought about it. What was different? How had I changed?

Do you know what I discovered? My whole network of friends and acquaintances had gradually changed! They were now all Christians like me. I hardly knew any lost people any more, and I certainly did not socialize with any!

You won't be surprised to learn that I was not the first person to make this observation. I was "merely a layperson" at the time, but it is true of ministers and laity alike. Nor am I the only one to suggest we must change this pattern.

> 📖 Many Christians, not least Christian preachers, simply do not know any out-and-out pagans. It is time they did. They should rearrange priorities and befriend some of them. When more and more people think of church as alien, the only way, humanly speaking, that people are going to attend public services and hear the gospel well articulated in the context of a worshiping community is if friends invite them. [86]

If you have no social relationships with non-Christians, to whom are you witnessing?

> 🖊 Interview four or five Christian acquaintances that you know have been instrumental in bringing people to the Lord. See if they have noticed this pattern early in their Christian life: they knew more non-Christians, but now, they know and interact with far fewer. Perhaps you can suggest they adopt a more proactive approach to the lost.

The overarching theme

Imagine trying to summarize the message of the whole Bible in one sentence. Tough assignment, isn't it? I tried to do it with this sentence: "God made us to have relationship with him, and our disobedience destroyed that relationship—but Jesus' death on the cross paid the penalty for our sin so that we could have relationship

---

[86] Carson, *The Gagging of God*. p.511.

with God again." OK, so it's a long sentence and maybe you could do better.

Now, how could you summarize the message of the whole Bible in a single word? This is an even tougher assignment! My answer may be inadequate, but the best answer I can find is the word "relationship." And I think this answer has value for every Christian.

For the sake of discussion, assume my answer is the best we can find. I believe God wants us to learn something about relationship with him through all of our human relationships. The first relationship people have is with their parents. And we should learn from this relationship what it means that God is a loving father. The next relationship we usually have is with siblings and friends, and perhaps we can even learn valuable lessons from our relationships with "enemies." I don't need to explain the rest of this illustration for you—just think about the lessons you might learn about relationship with God through your relationship with your spouse and your children.

But our culture fails to provide many people today with good relational experiences. Tell many people today that God loves them like a father or a mother, and they respond negatively. Many parents cannot identify with God disciplining us with love because they never disciplined their own children with love.

In spite of this, I am convinced that our best approach to witnessing and to explaining the Gospel are both contained in this one thought: relationship. But we have our work cut out for us.

Preparing your net

With whom do you have the most influence? Let's answer this question with the phrase "your network of friends and associates." I'll just call them *your network*. There are a dozen or so people that you will spend thirty minutes or more with each week and with whom you can talk about personal matters. Some of these are relatives, some are colleagues at school or work, some are neighbors, some are people with common interests or hobbies, with some you share common tasks, and with others you share common needs. Perhaps the following illustration will help you to visualize your network.

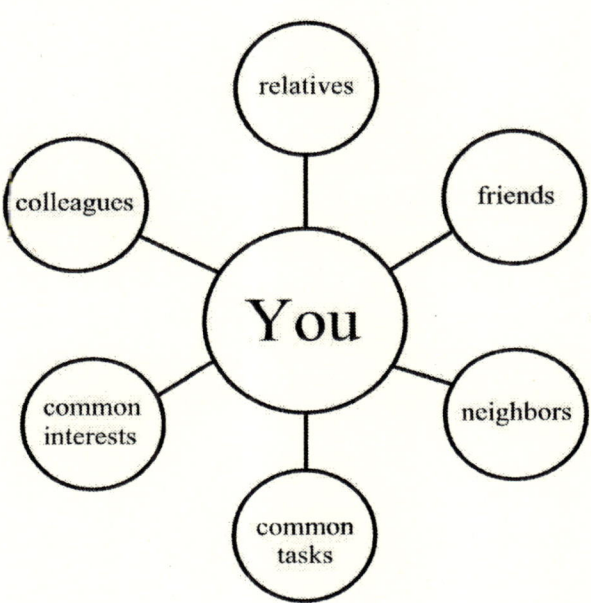

✎ Identify the people who are now part of your network. Write their names in your journal. Add to it as you think of others. Put an asterisk * by the non-Christians in your journal lists. You will use this information in the next chapter.

✎ The Appendix has a few exercises designed to help you develop witnessing strategies (pages 174-175). You might discuss these with friends before you make notes in your journal.

"Throw your net on the right side of the boat..."
John 21:6

Chapter 13
Let's Go Fishing!

What spoiled the fishing?

The opening chapter described "The Great Western Worldview Earthquake." Repeatedly in subsequent chapters I've argued that this "earthquake" has spoiled our fishing—that is, the strategies that brought people to faith before the "Worldview Earthquake" ushered in postmodernism are no longer effective. So let's consider strategies that are more effective.

Using your net

The entire book has been building to this chapter. Here you are challenged to take everything we've discussed and try to put it into practice. Intimidating, isn't it?

What is offered below is not a method or a formula for witnessing. It is a strategy to help you learn to build relationships with people as a foundation for effectively sharing the Gospel. It is not new, but quite old. I believe it is biblical.

Researchers tell us that the majority of all believers come to salvation through the influence of a friend or relative. Think of your own conversion. Whom did God use in your life? How did they influence you to trust in Jesus?

✎ Consider the following New Testament examples of relationships providing a forum for effective witness: Matthew 9:9-13; John 1:40-41,43-53; Acts 10:1-2, 24-26; 16:14-15; 16:31-34; 18:7-8. Describe or list the members of the network in each case.

The sad fact is that too many believers allow only other Christians to become part of their social network! Non-Christians are typically excluded. Can you think of ways you exclude non-Christians?

✎ Are non-Christians typically excluded from your social network? Has it always been this way, or did this develop only after you became a Christian? Does your church make this problem worse?

Our witnessing strategy must include extending our network to bring in nonbelievers. Accomplishing this will require some effort and prayer. You will be more likely to succeed if you will work with others who will hold you accountable—and whom you can hold accountable too. Are you willing?

Is this our pattern?

What usually happens to new converts? Does the local church typically train new converts to keep a network of non-Christians to whom we can witness? Not usually. Instead, the church quickly consumes as much time as it can and changes our whole circle of friends from non-Christians to Christians. I realize the advantage of this. Do you realize the disadvantage?

Why do many new converts quickly establish only Christian relationships to the exclusion of non-Christians? Perhaps they have heard sermons and Bible lessons based on these passages:

☦ *"If you belonged to the world, it would love you as its own. As it is, you do not belong to the world, but I have chosen you out of the world. That is why the world hates you." (John 15:19)*

☙ *Religion that God our Father accepts as pure and faultless is this: to look after orphans and widows in their distress and to keep oneself from being polluted by the world. (James 1:27)*

☙ *You adulterous people, don't you know that friendship with the world is hatred toward God? Anyone who chooses to be a friend of the world becomes an enemy of God. (James 4:4)*

☙ *Do not love the world or anything in the world. If anyone loves the world, the love of the Father is not in him. (1 John 2:15)*

Do these seem to indicate we should have nothing to do with the world (non-Christians)? But we should balance this with some other passages. In one of his prayers Jesus told his Father:

☦ *"I am coming to you now, but I say these things while I am still in the world, so that they may have the full measure of my joy within them. I have given them your word and the world has hated them, for they are not of the world any more than I am of the world. My prayer is not that you take them out of the world but that you protect them from the evil one." (John 17:13-15)*

And Paul instructed the church in Corinth with these words:

☙ *I have written you in my letter not to associate with sexually immoral people—not at all meaning the people of this world who are*

125

immoral, or the greedy and swindlers, or idolaters. In that case you would have to leave this world. But now I am writing you that you must not associate with anyone who calls himself a brother but is sexually immoral or greedy, an idolater or a slanderer, a drunkard or a swindler. (1 Corinthians 5:9-11)

As we disciple new converts, we must first help them make their current relationships with non-Christians safe so they won't be pulled back into a sinful lifestyle. But we must also help them learn how to develop new relationships with other non-Christians. If they don't, they will not have a pool of non-Christians to whom they can witness.

Go fishing

We need to go fishing. When I go fishing (literally), I must go where the fish are, I must know something about the fish I want to catch, and I have to use my fishing tackle. If I hope to catch any fish, I must have a fishing strategy.[87]

This is also true for witnessing. I must go where the lost are, I must understand how contemporary lost people think, I must use my witnessing tools, and I must have a strategy that fits the target audience.

Have you ever felt like the non-Christians so outnumber the believers that we have an impossible task? How can we ever hope to accomplish our mission? They're all around us. Let's not let a one of them get away.

✑ *The Lord is...patient with you, not wanting anyone to perish, but everyone to come to repentance. (2 Peter 3:9)*

If Christ does not want anyone to perish, shouldn't we have that same attitude?

We must learn to take advantage of what is left of God's image in the lost to help them see the light of the Gospel. Whatever interest a person has in spiritual things should be used to help them consider the claims of the Christ. Whatever longing for meaning in life remains should be taken advantage of.

---

[87] Like all metaphors, the picture of witnessing and winning the lost to Christ as "fishing" is imperfect. If you observe flaws, don't reject the metaphor—just recognize its limitations. Jesus introduced this metaphor when he told the fisherman brothers Peter and Andrew that if they would follow him, he would make them fishers of men. (Matthew 4:19 and Mark 1:17) They did, and he did.

We must become sensitive to the felt-needs of people so that we can point them to the only one who can genuinely meet those needs. The danger in trying to apply the Gospel to someone's felt need is that we might inadvertently distort the Gospel message. Carson correctly cautions us against this:

> 📖 Recognized or not, acknowledged or not, there is a profound and bitter emptiness at the hearts of many men and women in Western culture. I am not...suggesting that the Gospel be reshaped to become that which meets my emptiness: so crassly put, this would be one more way by which evangelicalism is only a whisker from affirming that God exists in order to meet my needs, as I perceive them. Human emptiness and moral confusion must be traced to its roots *in biblical theology;* only in that framework can the historic gospel truly address the underlying problem.[88]

We should help a person discover his or her need for forgiveness and recognize his or her need for the Savior.

At times we can also use the natural world to point the lost to the Creator. In Romans, Paul wrote:

> 🕊 *The wrath of God is being revealed from heaven against all the godlessness and wickedness of men who suppress the truth by their wickedness, since what may be known about God is plain to them, because God has made it plain to them. For since the creation of the world God's invisible qualities—his eternal power and divine nature—have been clearly seen, being understood from what has been made, so that men are without excuse. (Romans 1:18-20)*

Doesn't this seem to tell us that some knowledge of God can be gained from studying his creation?

> ✏ What aspects of God's nature do you see revealed in the natural world? List them. How might you use what you know about the natural world to point someone to the Creator (be specific).

Your fishing expedition

You may read this and conclude that you just don't have time to do this. And you are probably right—most of us don't have the time to do this. You might have to reorder your priorities to accomplish this. You will have to make time.

---

[88] Carson, *The Gagging of God.* p.495.

Below is an outline of what you are challenged to do. I hope you will interact with it.

1. Become part of a team

Join together with a small group (or at least one other person) that is convinced that this is the best strategy to reach the lost. If you cannot find such a group, create one yourself.

2. Find a "Mutual Accountability Partner"

Select someone to serve as your Mutual Accountability Partner (MAP)—preferably someone of the same gender. Ideally you will serve in this same capacity for him or her. Then follow the plan laid out below to accomplish these subgoals. Regularly discuss how you are succeeding and how you are failing with your MAP.

3. Pray with your MAP

Most Christians learned to pray by listening to other Christians pray. Space will not permit me to develop a biblical pattern of prayer, but you might read these passages: (Matthew 6:6-15; Luke 11:1-13; and Luke 18:1-8).

How do you pray for the lost? Do you just ask God to save your friends? While I do not want to discourage you from praying in this way, where in the Bible are we so instructed? Should the Bible inform our thinking of praying evangelistically? Friend and colleague Calvin Pincombe constructed a guide for biblical evangelistic prayer that forms an acrostic.

Calvin Pincombe's

FOCUSed New Testament Evangelistic Prayer Guide[89]

The focus of this guide is not on praying for unbelievers, but praying for Christians to be the witnesses that we are empowered to be (according to Acts 1:8 and Matthew 28:18-20). Here's how we will pray:

---

[89] Personal communiqué, Cal Pincombe, Central Bible College, Springfield, MO.

Fellow workers	**Pray** that God would supply laborers in the harvest (Matthew 9:38), and be willing to be the answer to your own prayer (Matthew 10:1).
Open doors	**Pray** that God would give you opportunities to share with those around you (Colossians 4:2-3). Make a list; pray specifically.
Courage	**Pray** for courage to step out of your comfort zone to build relationships with people listed above (Ephesians 6:19-20).
Utterance	**Pray** for the Spirit's guidance in knowing when, what, and how to share (Colossians 4:4; Ephesians 6:19).
Spreading of the Gospel	**Pray** that God would use you and your witnessing team to spread the Gospel. Pray that you would see the faithfulness of his strength and protection from the evil one (2 Thessalonians 3:1-3).

*Devote yourselves to prayer…*Colossians 4:2

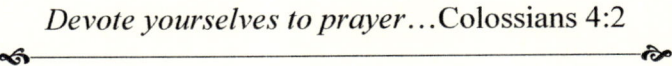

4. Expand your network

Using FOCUSed prayer, ask the Holy Spirit to lead you to people that you might include in your network and with whom you can begin building a relationship. Write the names of these people in your journal.

> ✎ Do you see how the FOCUS Evangelistic Prayer Guide connects to our strategy? Re-read it and identify which of the five points especially connects to our strategy for expanding our network of friends.

Choose (with God's guidance) just one or two people (maximum of three) to start with that you will strive to incorporate into your network. Highlight their names in your journal. Pray daily for each person you have chosen as a candidate for your expanded network of friends.

5. Develop a relationship with your new non-Christian friend

Using everything you know about friendship, develop a trusting, long-term relationship with one or two of these people (maximum of three). Invest time in doing things together. Engage in honest, open conversations that build trust.

Work with the Holy Spirit to discover activities you can use to develop your relationship with these people. Then be a friend—show yourself friendly. Here are a few things you can do *together* to help incorporate new people into your network:

- Share a meal at your home or theirs
- Play a table game or a sport together
- Throw a block party
- Take a short trip together
- Celebrate a birthday or an anniversary
- Organize a cookout (e.g., Memorial Day, Fourth of July, Labor Day, block party)
- Attend a concert together
- Share a vegetable garden
- Repair or maintain a car
- Help with some other project
- Get to know the parents of your children's friends

✎ Try to expand this list of things to *do with people* to develop your network.

Here are some things you can do *for* them:

- Provide a meal during a family crisis
- Watch house, feed pets, water plants, take in mail during vacation
- Baby-sit their children while they have a night out
- Lend tools
- Help with a project

Don't forget what Paul taught in Romans 12:9: "Love must be sincere." Insincerity will destroy all else you do to develop a relationship.

✎ Try to expand this list of things to do for people to enlarge your network. Choose things you can do *with* and *for* each of these people to help build relationship with them. Write their names, these activities, and possible dates to do them in your journal.
---

6. Discover where your friend is in the process of coming to faith

Becoming a Christian is not only an event, it is also a process. As you cultivate a relationship with this person (or these people), try to estimate where he or she is in this process of coming to faith in Jesus. Consider the following helpful (but limited and general) scale:

9	Hostile to Christianity and Christians
8	Distorted view of Gospel message
7	Unaware, ignorant of the Gospel
6	Open to being a friend with a Christian
5	Open to hearing the Gospel message
4	Understands the Gospel message
3	Recognizes need of a Savior
2	Willing to repent and believe
1	Receives Christ as Lord and Savior

Where would you place your new friends on this scale?[90] (The numbers merely facilitate discussion and have no other significance.) Where your friend is on this scale should help determine what you tell him or her. If she were at number 7, you would want to help her gain a correct view of the Gospel. If he were at number 4, you would want to help him accept his personal need for a Savior.

> ✎ Would you want to tell your friend your own salvation story if he were at number 9? Does it matter? Why?

7. Share your testimony

Now, based on what you learn about this friend, find ways to tell this friend how you came to faith in Christ and what God has done in your life since that experience. If you wrote out your testimony as suggested in an earlier chapter, how would you modify it to witness to this friend?

---

[90] The idea of a scale like this is certainly not original with me, several have been developed. One such scale can be found in White's "Evangelism in a Postmodern World" in *The Challenge of Postmodernism.*

Perhaps you can provide an opportunity for other Christian friends to testify to this friend too. Be led by the Spirit in choosing when you should invite this non-Christian friend to attend a church worship service with you. Don't forget—you want her to come to faith, not to church!

Not a guaranteed formula for success

Don't think that this is a surefire plan that you can just use 1-2-3-4 and, *voilà!* success. Using this strategy will help develop your abilities, and you may use it more than once before you see a friend come to faith. But this strategy is consistent with the New Testament pattern.

Is the witnessing strategy you have been using better than this one?

Paul's prayer for the Christians in Ephesus might encourage you:

- *I pray that out of his glorious riches he may strengthen you with power through his Spirit in your inner being, so that Christ may dwell in your hearts through faith. And I pray that you, being rooted and established in love, may have power, together with all the saints, to grasp how wide and long and high and deep is the love of Christ, and to know this love that surpasses knowledge—that you may be filled to the measure of all the fullness of God.*

- *Now to him who is able to do immeasurably more than all we ask or imagine, according to his power that is at work within us, to him be glory in the church and in Christ Jesus throughout all generations, for ever and ever! Amen. (Ephesians 3:14-21)*

"If you have raced with men on foot and they have worn you out, how can you compete with horses?"
Jeremiah 12:5

Chapter 14
You Gonna Fish? Or Cut Bait?

Never forget your source

We should do all we can to learn how to effectively witness to non-Christians, but we must never forget who makes us fruitful in everything we do. The Apostle Paul was very skilled, and yet he described his service to God like this:

📖 *Not that we are competent in ourselves to claim anything for ourselves, but our competence comes from God. He has made us competent as ministers of a new covenant—not of the letter but of the Spirit; for the letter kills, but the Spirit gives life. (2 Corinthians 3:5-6)*

This is usually easier to keep in mind as you are learning how to share your faith. After you become used to God using you in this way, however, it is easier to forget this fact and start relying on your abilities.

The eternal chain

You will never know the chain reaction your witnessing might initiate. Consider just this one illustration.

📖 A Sunday school teacher, a Mr. Kimball, in 1858, led a Boston shoe clerk to give his life to Christ.

📖 The clerk, Dwight L. Moody, became an evangelist. In England in 1879, he awakened evangelistic zeal in the heart of Fredrick B. Meyer, pastor of a small church.

📖 F. B. Meyer, preaching to an American college campus, brought to Christ a student named J. Wilbur Chapman.

📖 Chapman, engaged in YMCA work, employed a former baseball player, Billy Sunday, to do evangelistic work.

📖 Billy Sunday held a revival in Charlotte, North Carolina. A group of local men were so enthusiastic afterward that they planned another evangelistic campaign, bringing Mordecai Hamm to town to preach.

> 📖 During Hamm's revival, a young man responded to the Gospel and Billy Graham yielded his life to Christ.
>
> 📖 Only eternity will reveal the impact of that Sunday school teacher Kimball witnessing to a shoe store clerk.[91]

Do you know anyone who came to Christ through the ministry of Billy Graham? Then add his or her name to this list of people affected by that shoe store clerk almost 150 years ago!

The value of apologetics

Should you develop a personal apologetic? Should a Christian learn to explain why she believes what she believes? By now you know that I answer "Yes!" Although some suggest that an apologetic rarely wins a lost person to the Lord, your apologetic can help you see that faith is reasonable and has a rational basis. But some agree with Alister McGrath in his assertion that apologetics can also help you build a bridge from where a non-Christian is to saving faith in Christ.[92]

A variety of witnessing aids

Here is a list of ideas that I've accumulated over years of witnessing and observing that might help you to witness better.

1. Present Jesus as Savior. Never portray Jesus as a Mr. Fix-It who will solve all of life's problems if a person will just become a Christian. Having financial problems? Become a Christian and Jesus will solve them. Marriage problems? Medical problems? Emotional problems? Become a Christian and all these problems will disappear—so some Christians like to say.

   This is not biblical, and if you persuade someone to do this, you are setting him or her up for a fall. Instead, warn them that if they will receive Christ as Lord and Savior, they can expect an attack from the devil. God does not promise to *remove* all of the Christian's problems, instead he promises to *be with us* through all of life's problems!

2. Perceive salvation not only as an event, but also as a process. Most Evangelicals typically view salvation only as an event. But the Bible

---

[91] "The Ripple Effect," found on several web sites including this one: "Who? Me? An Evangelist?" www.whome.net/training/articles/ripple.htm.

[92] McGrath uses this concept in his book *Intellectuals Don't Need God & Other Modern Myths*.

speaks of salvation in the past tense, present tense, and future tense. How could seeing salvation as a process change your witnessing strategy?

3. Don't try to do it all in one day. Be prepared for the long haul. Building a relationship to set the stage for witnessing takes time. Pace yourself.

4. Even though most postmodernists won't listen to you quote the Bible, you can include what the Bible says in your witness—either directly or as a paraphrase. As Paul wrote,

> *"So then faith comes by hearing, and hearing by the word of God." (Romans 10:17, New King James Version)*

And the Prophet Isaiah quoted God as saying

> *"So is my word that goes out from my mouth: It will not return to me empty, but will accomplish what I desire and achieve the purpose for which I sent it." (Isaiah 55:11)*

In your testimony, tell people how you experienced what the Bible says everyone who becomes a Christian will experience.

5. Because most postmodernists will not listen to the Bible with respect, your consistent life is crucial. Years ago we reminded ourselves of the importance of living the Christian life with this proverb: "Your life may be the only 'Bible' some people ever read." Postmodernists usually value relationships more than they value facts or arguments. So the pulpit evangelist is often not as effective in reaching a person in our postmodern culture as a friend who nurtures an authentic relationship.

6. Find a Christian friend to team up with to witness with you. In the Gospels, Jesus sent the disciples out two by two, and in the Revelation, John saw two witnesses in the end time. You can witness by yourself, but most people will be more effective witnessing with a friend.

7. One of the best things you can do to learn how to share a personal testimony is to go with a witnessing Christian. You can be the "silent partner" at first. Watch what he or she does. Consider what you would do differently. After a few trips, perhaps your friend would be the silent partner and go with you while you witness to a friend with whom you have been building a relationship.

8. Be ready to admit the errors of the past and present. Christianity was soft on slavery in many places. Even today, many Christians have not taken a strong stand against racism. Some Christians have polluted the environment in order to increase corporate profits. But the errors of some Christian groups do not invalidate the truth of the Gospel of Jesus Christ. Don't try to excuse the mistakes of other Christians. Just don't let these sidetrack you from the more critical issues!

9. Don't pretend you have the answer to every question. You don't even know all the questions. Feel free to admit this. But you do know the answer to the ultimate question, and his name is Jesus.
10. Don't assume that Christian symbols and metaphors (e.g., the Cross, Christ's blood, etc.) mean something or the right thing to your hearers.

> ✎ Explain the meaning of some of the Christian symbols. What does it mean that the blood of Jesus will save you? Is this magic blood? Is the cross of Christ magic, too?

11. Don't ignore the Old Testament. Use Old Testament history to explain the significance of Jesus as Messiah. Don't assume your hearers will already know these stories. The Old Testament is also a rich source for developing a Christian social ethic.

> ✎ List several Old Testament stories you think would be useful in explaining the person and work of Jesus Christ.

12. If you are going to stay culturally aware, you need to read. Either go to the library or subscribe to a couple of popular magazines and stay familiar with what people in your culture are thinking. Read the local newspaper to see what the people in your local subculture think. Consider what popular music, television, and movies reveal about our culture. Convert some of your TV time into reading time.t

> ✎ List the periodicals you read to stay aware of your culture. Does this need to change?

13. When you find yourself disagreeing with a non-Christian, remember to disagree respectfully. Notice how Peter ended his admonition:

> ❧ *Always be prepared to give an answer to everyone who asks you to give the reason for the hope that you have. But do this with gentleness and respect, keeping a clear conscience. (1 Peter 3:15-16)*

14. I wish it were unnecessary to remind people of the importance of not breaking a confidence, but too many times I've been told things that I know have been told in confidence. Sometimes the confidence is understood, not stated. If people you are witnessing to feel like you have betrayed their confidence, they will probably reject the Gospel message.
15. Sometimes people confide an embarrassing experience. Then, later, they wish they had not spoken so candidly—they shared too much, too early. When this happens, they often react by withdrawing. If you have this experience, you may have to gently reassure that person that you think no less of them because of what they shared with you.

16. Church leaders—pastors, staff members, teachers—all church leaders, must lead the way in setting the example in evangelism. Without this, church members will not believe it is a matter of top priority. Invite your church leaders to get involved with you in witnessing projects.

17. A warm, friendly spirit is invaluable in witnessing. You want that lost person to perceive you as a friend, not an enemy. When talking about the Lord, you may be passionate, but your tone of voice, your facial expressions, your body language, your use of eye contact, even your use of the person's name—everything about you—must be attractive, not repulsive. A smile is a great asset. Don't overlook these.

18. Ethnic groups are growing in most urban metropolitan areas. Don't be timid to witness to people of a different ethnicity, but carefully respect cultural differences. If you want to build a cross-cultural relationship, take the time to learn as much as you can about that culture. Don't forget: you want this person to place his or her faith in Jesus, not abandon his or her ethnic group to become part of your ethnic group.

19. Never forget what your life and worldview were like before you became a Christian.

20. One of the simplest, yet most important things you can do, is simply be yourself. Don't try to be like someone you admire, just be genuinely yourself. Don't try to copy someone else's personality, let your own personality show. Don't artificially adopt the jargon of the person to whom you are witnessing.

21. No matter how positive you are that the person you are witnessing to is wrong about a fact or a point, and no matter how sure you are that you are right, never act like an arrogant know-it-all. Always be humble and recognize that you are often wrong too. You are trying to win a friend, not win an argument.

22. In order to witness, you will at times have to disagree; but you must learn how to disagree without being disagreeable (insulting, arrogant, etc.). Be respectful and courteous when you must disagree. St. Augustine said, "In essentials, unity; in non-essentials, liberty; in all things, charity." Jesus said that people would know that we are his disciples by our love—not by our great arguments (John 13:35).

23. You can hardly overemphasize the fact that salvation through faith in Christ Jesus is always by his grace, never earned by the believer. Even Christians who know this often do not live like it.

24. Sooner or later you will have to be prepared to answer the false teachings of some of the more common cults (e.g., the Mormons and the Jehovah's Witnesses). Typically the errors these cults make have to do with the person and work of Christ Jesus, the Bible as the sole authority in matters of faith and practice, and/or who can correctly interpret the

Bible. You would do well to prepare yourself for an encounter with a cult member. A few resources are listed in the bibliography.

25. Avoid answering questions with "prepackaged" answers. Clichés and gimmicks are often poor communicators of the Gospel message. Bumper sticker Christianity will not sustain a person through the hardships of life. I know this by personal experience. If you don't know this, if you live long enough, you will too.

26. Timing is so crucial that we must seek the leading of the Holy Spirit in this respect. I recall reading a story of a barber who loved to witness. Once after lathering a face to shave, while he ran the straight razor over the strop, he asked his customer, "Sir, are you prepared to meet your Creator?" Of course the man immediately ran from the barbershop.

27. Don't let vulgar language from a lost person repulse you. If you rebuke them for language you find offensive, they may turn a deaf ear to your witness.

Remember who you are!

One of the most valuable assets in witnessing can be recognition of who you are in Christ Jesus. What does the Bible say about us? We Christians are:

The children of God	John 1:12
The saved	John 10:9
Jesus' brother and sisters	Mark 3:31-35
The people of God	Hebrews 4:9
Joint heirs	Romans 8:17
Sons of the living God	Romans 9:26
Citizens of heaven	Philippians 3:20
The household of faith	1 Timothy 3:15
God's elect	Titus 1:1
A chosen people	1 Peter 2:9
A royal priesthood	1 Peter 2:9
A holy nation	1 Peter 2:9
A people belonging to God	1 Peter 2:9
Brothers	1 John 2:10; 4:21
Priests	Revelation 5:10

You might be "nobody" in the eyes of some people, but you are so valuable to God, that he sent his only Son to die to pay for your sins and placed his own Holy Spirit in you! You just cannot get any more important than that.

Don't get your eyes on some great leader and wish you could do the things he or she is doing. You can become so focused on who you are *not*, that you fail to become the person God wants you to be.

Paul used a military metaphor when he told his "true son in the faith":

📖 *No one serving as a soldier gets involved in civilian affairs—he wants to please his commanding officer. (2 Timothy 2:4)*

We would do well to accept the US Army's former motto as our own, too: "Be all that you can be!" And the only way to do that is to let God be your commanding officer and have complete control of your life.

The big challenge

I think one of the biggest challenges facing the Church in this decade is how to actively demonstrate God's love to sinners without appearing to condone sin. Instead, we Christians are perceived as hating sinners. Our world sees us as hating gays and lesbians, divorcees, adulterers, pornographers, drunks, drug addicts, abortionists and those who have had abortions. I fear too often we deserve this charge.

For example, Taylor says that the Church has failed to respond to homosexuals and the AIDS problem as well as it eventually responded to those in favor of abortion:

> 📖 We have failed so far to respond as well to homosexuals. We have not been in the frontlines in the fight against AIDS, just as we were not in the struggle against racism. How differently would conservative Christianity be perceived today if we had been the first and most passionate of those offering practical help to AIDS sufferers? The bulk of our response—verbal and nonverbal, literal and symbolic—suggests that we hate the sinner every bit as much as the sin. This is the story we hear from gays in our pews as much as from those in the parades. We can say it isn't so; but talk is cheap. We do not have to affirm homosexuals in their homosexuality, as our culture insists, but we do have to love them, and we haven't yet figured out how to do that.[93]

---

[93] Taylor, "Are You Tolerant?" *Christianity Today.* January 11, 1999, p.52.

Jesus was known as a friend of sinners and was criticized for socializing with sinners. (Matthew 11:19 and Luke 7:34.) How unlike him are we. Often Christians are perceived as the foe of sinners.

✎ In your journal, suggest several ways Christians can correct this without compromising our integrity or witness.

Years ago I had a close personal friend who was the pastor of an independent, evangelical church. One day he told me that several of his church members were becoming quite active in the anti-abortion movement. "I don't want our church to become known as 'the church in town that is against abortion,'" he told me. I was quite surprised.

"I thought you were against abortion," I replied, trying to remain poised.

"I am," he said.

"Then why did you say that?"

"If we become known as the church against abortion, will people who have had abortions come to us? Will people who are struggling with decisions about abortions seek us out?" he asked me.

"Probably not," was my thoughtful reply.

"I would like for us to become known as the church in this town full of people who love sinners."

I do not have an answer, but somehow we must communicate God's love to sinners without seeming to condone sin. Perhaps you can help me learn how to put this into practice.

Putting it all together

So what have we learned? Let's review.

♦ We've described modernism and postmodernism and how they have shaped the worldview of typical Westerners.

♦ We've seen that the way Christians think has also been negatively influenced by postmodernism—and it affects how we witness.

♦ We've considered many elements of witnessing: why we witness, why we fail to witness, responding to atheists, and New Testament examples of witnessing.

♦ We've looked at the functions of the Bible, the Holy Spirit, supernatural events, good works, fasting, reasoning, love, and prayer in witnessing.

- We've tried to understand what the Gospel is and what a witness is—and is not—arguing that New Testament witnessing always has the person and work of Jesus as its focus.
- Then we tried to consider the often unique problems of witnessing to postmodernists.
- We considered some biblical examples that should give us insights into witnessing.
- Nowhere did I suggest that you could learn and use a formula or a method to witness. Instead I emphasized that a strategy for witnessing should:
    1. Proceed from who you are: a compassionate Christian controlled by the Holy Spirit of God.
    2. Be built on a genuine relationship that includes trust.
    3. Discover who this lost person is, his or her values, worldview, etc.
    4. Demonstrate God's love through good works to them.
    5. Focus on the person and work of the historical Jesus of Nazareth.
    6. Over a period of time, present a biblical worldview, a biblical description of God, of humans and our predicament, and of God's offer of salvation through Christ Jesus' death and resurrection.
    7. Allow God's Spirit to use you and others to communicate the message of the Gospel to them at the right time and in the right way (contextualization).
- We considered spiritual disciplines that will help us mature in the faith.
- We affirmed and differentiated the biblical role of evangelists from the command for all Christians to witness.
- You were forewarned about a variety of common mistakes.
- Witnessing must proceed from who we are, not from some learned method of evangelism.
- We must learn how to identify with the lost while at the same time we live a life of holiness that completely identifies us with the Lord.
- We must become proactive in building a network of relationships with non-Christians to whom we can witness.

♦ Finally, we are challenged to use all that we've gained to go fishing!

I think that when the truth in this prayer becomes real in your life...

🕊 *May the God of hope fill you with all joy and peace as you trust in him, so that you may overflow with hope by the power of the Holy Spirit. (Romans 15:13)*

...then these words of Jesus will also be true of you:

✞ *You will receive power when the Holy Spirit comes on you; and you will be my witnesses...to the ends of the earth. (Acts 1:8)*

Appendix

Summary of Stephen Eyre's

Defeating the Dragons of the World, IVP, 1987

(Connect this to page 14.)

One of the most practical features of Eyre's book is the discipline that he suggests you can use to defeat each of these dragons (false values). I highly recommend reading the book (even if it is just a little bit dated) because it helps to highlight the prevailing cultural values during the 1970s through at least the 1980s. This may help you better understand how we arrived at our current postmodern state.

Materialism

Summary statement	Matter is all that matters.
Leads you to think you are	...what you own" (possess)
Presents a deformed view	...of the world
False value based on	Your worth is determined on the basis of what you own.
Biblical value	Christ in you
Discipline to defeat it	Meditation

Activism

Summary statement	Life must be filled with action.
Leads you to think you are	...what you do" (produce)
Presents a deformed view	...of work
False value based on	Your worth is measured by what you do—by what you produce.
Biblical value	God makes fruitful
Discipline to defeat it	Two-way prayer

Individualism

Summary statement	You can depend on no one but yourself.
Leads you to think you are	...sufficient without other people"
Presents a deformed view	...of self
False value based on	You are the sole source of determining your worth.
Biblical value	Created in His image
Discipline to defeat it	Community

Conformism

Summary statement	Recognition by others is a necessity.
Leads you to think you are	...who others recognize you to be"
Presents a deformed view	...of others
False value based on	Others are the sole source of determining your worth.
Biblical value	God knows you
Discipline to defeat it	Solitude

Relativism

Summary statement	What you believe doesn't matter, as long as you believe something.
Leads you to think you are	...whatever you choose to believe"
Presents a deformed view	...of truth
False value based on	No absolutes; your worth is determined by the values you choose.
Biblical value	God's Word is truth
Discipline to defeat it	Bible study

Secularism

Summary statement	Religion is all right in its place.
Leads you to think you are	...sufficient without God"
Presents a deformed view	...of God
False value based on	Religious values apply only on Sunday and in church.
Biblical value	God is always present
Discipline to defeat it	Stewardship

Sensualism[94]

Summary statement	If it feels good, do it. (If it doesn't, don't!)
Leads you to think you are	...what you feel"
Presents a deformed view	...of pleasure and pain; (all our feelings and emotions, including excitement and fun)
False value based on	Worth is determined by the amount of pleasure or pain someone brings
Biblical value	God's Presence (relationship, worship) gives pleasure, and He has provided many pleasures, but...
Discipline to defeat it	Self-control

---

[94] This false value of Sensualism was not in Eyre's book but was added by Steve Badger in collaboration with Stephen Eyre.

Cognitive Reflections of a Dissonant Gen-Xer

By Rich Tatum

(Connect this to page 21.)

Dear Steve,

Thanks for sending me a copy of your manuscript. Here are some random thoughts and observations I had while reading the first chapter—this is not a critique. I think my reactions confirm the appropriateness of your material for folks like me, and perhaps your readers will benefit from a view into a fellow reader's reaction.

I am discovering that postmodern thinking is far more pervasive than we "modernist" Christians would like to think it is. The more I learn about postmodernism the more I think, "Wow, I didn't know I thought that way." This is creepy, and too often an uncomfortable cognitive dissonance surprises me when I find myself caught between modernity and postmodernism.

Let me give you an example. I have been deeply involved in the Internet and with managing online content for several years now. Not long ago, while working for the national headquarters of my church's denomination, I was charged with bringing a website content management system online. To accomplish this, I worked closely with a thoroughly postmodern Web designer/programmer named Andy. In describing his philosophy of Web content management and programming Andy told me, "Don't impose your own view of structure on the content on your website. Your site visitors should discover the structure that best suits their interests, and your content should 'arrange' itself according to structures and patterns that arise naturally out of the content itself and how your visitors use it."

Andy further described how imposing a rigid hierarchy, outline, or structure on our Web content is arrogant: how could we possibly know what information is most important to all of the users who come to our site? For instance, by featuring corporate news on the front page we were making an assumption that news is what our readers were interested in and, worse, forces all users to conform to our arrogantly presumptuous scheme of "the way things ought to be."

The more Andy described his way of thinking, the more I realized it resonated with me, until I started to think about our Web project from the perspective of our denominational leadership—thoroughly modernist men. I imagined a board meeting where I insisted that a front page presentation of our core doctrines is inherently arrogant and that "information should organize itself." I also imagined being laughed out of a job—quickly! Then I realized, "But wait, there *is* content that should be pointed out as having greater importance; the Bible makes it clear that some ideas get priority, no matter what, and that letting 'information organize itself' is nothing more than letting chaos rule!"

I finally sorted this all out in my head and arrived at a quasi postmodernist/modernist means of managing content on the denominational website, but not without thinking long about the nature of my denomination, its mission and message, and what the visitors to our website really wanted. A modernist publisher (or webmaster) will choose a topic of importance, craft it into a highly individualized presentation, and then publish it (sometimes with little regard for its "market value.") A postmodernist, however, will declare "Information wants to be free!" and will gleefully throw any and every scrap of information onto a website and "let the users sort it out."

A modernist would employ a thoroughly edited and controlled "Letters to the Editor" column. A postmodernist would employ an unmoderated message board. Even better—a chat room: ever fluid, never archived, constantly undergoing transformation. No absolutes. As a person stuck between modernity and postmodernity, I find myself enjoying both.

Okay, so that's one slice of my thoughts. I'm more postmodern than I realize. Parts of my worldview are modernistic, but parts are postmodern. The part of me which is postmodern enjoys Twin Peaks, Nike commercials, the first very Macintosh commercial (aired during the 1984 Super Bowl, featuring a female Olympian hurling a hammer and destroying the gray, washed-out, status quo), virtual reality, role playing games, *The Usual Suspects*, *Sixth Sense*, and *The Matrix*. The part of me that is modern yearns for unifying ideas, vainly searches for meaning in obscure collegiate literature, and rejects Southern-style rhetorical preaching. May God save me from my own cognitive dissonance!

Another observation I had reading this first chapter is that it seems "love" is the perfect antidote to postmodernism. I believe Walter Martin said it best in the preface to *Kingdom of the Cults*. Essentially, people don't choose faith-systems because they make logical sense. Instead, people choose to align themselves with a faith system because of how it makes them feel about themselves. In other words, people join the Mormon church not because it "makes perfect sense," but because when you're around a group of Mormons you feel loved and accepted.

This is an important point: people usually "join" the church not because we Christians won the debate or used superior logic: people join because they were loved in. Thus, the churches that grow the fastest, probably speak to that postmodern need for community better than the churches that focus solely on the intellectual or liturgical aspects of faith.

When I taught my campus ministry students about evangelism, I always stressed relationship over and above "winning" arguments. I took as my example Jesus, who was most intolerant of falsely religious hypocrites. Yet his most loving words were reserved for the sinners who couldn't follow God's moral code because they didn't know it and hadn't accepted it. Judging by the results of Jesus' love, I conclude:

"A loving Christian is never at the mercy of a lost sinner with a good argument!"

Speaking of arguments: in my discussions with postmodernists, I have found that, despite the philosophical influence of Nietzsche, Foucault, Derrida and others on postmodernism, most people have never heard of these dudes much less read their work. Instead, I find that the "common" postmodern worldview has its roots wrapped around rotted theories of evolution. Which makes sense: if you accept evolution as a starting premise, the logical conclusion is postmodernism and relativism. If evolutionary theories are true, humans are ultimately no better than any animal, and morality is nothing more than ritualized agreements not to hurt each other into extinction. So, I have found that challenging that presumption is often an effective way to erode the "mind screen" the postmodern victim hides behind.

147

I also thought about your comments on style vs. substance. I have also observed that postmodernism elevates art over discourse. You could pick up any anthology of poems today or listen to the pop radio for an hour and find an artist who willingly ascribes no meaning to their "art" because the meaning is in the eye of the beholder. Who could read James Joyce's stream-of-consciousness work and mistake him for a modernist? In a postmodern world a "Piss Christ" photograph and a "Dung Madonna" painting don't have to have any objective meaning invested in them by the artist.[95] In a postmodern world Christians are thought silly for getting lathered up over what the artist fully believes amounts to "nothing" because meaning is created in the minds of the audience, not the artist.

Similarly, body art (tattoos, piercings, and words) elevate "art" over the value of the "meat" that is the human body (almost a return to gnosticism and mystery religions). Body art is viewed as helping the flesh transcend its mundane nature as the container for the intellect and becomes transformed by the art itself into a message. Of course, if you're postmodernist, what that message is, is anybody's guess.

And your guess would be as good as mine. Know what I mean?
Rich Tatum
Carol Stream, IL

---

[95] This is a reference to a controversial work by Andres Serrano entitled "Piss Christ" (1989) and a collage by Chris Ofili titled "The Holy Virgin Mary" that incorporated elephant feces (1996).

An Open Letter to My Postmodern Friends

(Connect this to page 32.)

February 2001

Dear Friend,

I hope you will bear with me if this letter is a little long. I'll try to keep it as short as possible, but there is so much I want and need to tell you, that I know it won't be a one-pager. You told me some things about you—and I have observed other things—that may allow me to share some helpful thoughts with you. Well, we'll see.

In a nutshell, you are a child of your culture. Don't be offended—so am I (a product of my culture). We are all—to some extent anyway.

Part of maturation consists of identifying the false aspects of our culture and rejecting them—and also finding truths missing from our cultural fabric and embracing them. And that's what I want to talk about in this letter. I guess I could call what follows "Lies Our Culture Taught Us to Embrace as Truth." (In this letter, I will not try to name every cultural falsehood, just a few of the more important ones.)

In what follows, I will not introduce each statement with "In my opinion…" I'm writing this, so it should go without saying that it is my opinion. But be aware that the opinions that follow were reached over decades of observing, of reading, of discussing with others (some of whom agreed, some of whom disagreed), and of prayerfully thinking. Also, none of these opinions is private—many other people share these conclusions. I doubt even one of the ideas that follow is original with me.

The list that follows describes the results of gradual changes that have been occurring in our Western Culture over about the last 50 years—approximately since the end of the Second World War. Some of the changes began even before that. Suffice it to say that the world (culture) you grew up in was radically different from the world that your father and I grew up in. (I'll explain this a little more at the end.) So let me get to it…

149

Lies Our Culture Taught Us to Embrace as Truth

Lie #1. God—the God of the Bible—does not exist.

Not only does God not exist, the concept of God is superfluous—not necessary or useful. We don't need God—we don't need to believe in God. Why? Modern science has rendered the concept of God as useless.

The idea of God was simply used to explain things people did not understand a long time ago (in a pre-scientific era). Ancient, ignorant people explained many things by appealing to God and other spirits. Today we know better.

Lie #2. There is no such thing as absolute truth.

Our culture claims that all truth is subjective and relative. What is true for you may not be true for me. Truth is only in the mind of the individual.

On the other hand, while claiming that there are no absolute truths, our culture also tells us that all religions contain some truth, and all are merely different paths to the same destination, to the same God. So which religion you choose—if any—hardly matters.

Some say science is our best, maybe only, hope of acquiring useful truth (even if these truths are not universal), but science is not able to test religious claims.

Lie #3. There are no metanarratives.

Closely connected to this second lie (that there is no such thing as absolute truth) is the idea that there are no metanarratives. A metanarrative is a "story" (account, narrative) that is universally true—true for all humans everywhere.

So this lie would have us believe that all "truths" are culturally bound. One culture (or subculture) may embrace one truth, while another embraces another truth. All of these so-called metanarratives are really only local narratives, because they are not universal.

Further, anyone who proclaims a metanarrative (a universal truth) is merely trying to use it to dominate and control another group of people.

Lie #4. People are able to solve all of our own problems.

It does not matter that God does not exist—we don't need Him anyway, because we humans are able to solve all of our own problems. This idea grew out of the philosophies of "The Enlightenment" with its excessive confidence in human reason. This is summed up at the end of poet William Ernest's *Invictus*. He wrote: "I am the master of my fate; I am the captain of my soul." (*Invictus* means *Unconquered One*.)

That people are able in themselves and by themselves to solve all of humankind's problems is the message proclaimed by the "secular humanists" for at least the past 70 years, and most Americans embrace it either consciously or subconsciously.

Lie #5. People have a right to happiness.

Every schoolboy knows that "life, liberty, and the pursuit of happiness" is the God-given right of every American. And for many people, happiness depends on our appearance, our possessions, and our pleasures. Since this is our *right*, anything that limits our happiness, then, is *wrong*.

Lie #6. Complete personal freedom is prerequisite to true happiness.

Any and all restraints on my freedom rob me of my patriotic, inalienable right to life, liberty and the pursuit of happiness. No one has the right to function as an authority over me—my thoughts or my behavior. In whatever way my freedom is diminished, my happiness is diminished too. I must be free—free to be me!

Lie #7. The existence of all life on earth—including humans—is just by chance.

How else, if there is no God? Science (they argue) has eliminated all rational arguments 1. in favor of the existence of God and 2. against atheistic evolution. Scientists claim to know that all life is just the result of random happenings. Life, they claim, arose spontaneously from non-life, and then evolved into the variety of life that exists today. Humans are just another animal species that evolved from other life forms.

Did you notice how these lies are all interconnected? Together they form *a web that traps us* into a worldview that prevents us from discovering the truth about ourselves and the Creator.

By embracing these lies as truth, many people are deceived into reaching certain conclusions (either as conscious, thought-out conclusions, or just as general feelings that they never consciously recognize). Let me summarize for you some conclusions provoked by these cultural lies.

Those Seven Cultural Lies Promote These False Conclusions

Conclusion #1. Any person who embraces an absolute truth (metanarrative) is wrong.

Not only are these people wrong, but also they are trying to dominate and control some group of people. And conservative Christian groups all fall into this category, because they claim a biblical metanarrative. We should ignore all people making religious claims; they are all grasping for power in order to dominate others.

Since there is no God, the Bible cannot be the Word of God. But just as important, since it claims a metanarrative, the Bible cannot be trusted as truth. It may contain some interesting or useful stories, but that's all—it is not authoritative.

Conclusion #2. The only things we can trust as true are things that have scientific proof.

Even though there are no absolute truths, science is our only hope of finding even local truth. The successes of science like engineering (including flight—even to the moon) and modern medicine (including surgery and a long list of drugs) demonstrate the superiority of science over all other sources of knowledge. No other method or discipline can offer useful knowledge, that is knowledge worth embracing—only science.

Conclusion #3. People have little, if any, intrinsic value.

If I do not have much value, other people don't have much value either. This makes it easy for me to accept abortion and euthanasia. But then, I don't feel too good about myself. If all the cultural lies above are really true, what value does a human life have? Only the worth that I deem it has.

Conclusion #4. If I don't feel "happy" all the time, something is wrong with me.

Happiness becomes the value by which I measure the value of everything else. This drives me to spend most of my time and money pursuing pleasure with the hope that this one added pleasure will make me feel "happy" and give me a sense of self-worth. So sexual pleasure, drug induced euphoria, and the joys of ownership are all embraced as acceptable roads to the happiness that I deserve.

Conclusion #5. I am able to solve all of my problems.

I may need some help from a friend, but I don't need supernatural help. It really doesn't matter if I think I need supernatural help—there is no God to help me. In any case, humans have all we need to solve all of our problems.

Conclusion #6. Anything that would limit my freedom is wrong and my enemy.

This is what religion—especially Christianity—wants to do: give me a list of things that I must not do. The Christian church wants to limit my freedom, so it is my enemy. God wants to limit my freedom, and the Bible wants to limit my freedom, so they are wrong.

Some people have told me that they fear becoming a Christian because God might require them to marry someone they find repulsive or go to the jungles of Africa as a missionary or do something else that they would find revolting—or worse yet, boring.

Conclusion #7. My life has no real meaning or purpose.

Since there is no God, there is no Creator, and we are here as the result of random chance. Thus my life, in fact any person's life, will have only the meaning that I (he or she) give it.

Did you notice how all these ideas are also interconnected? (More of that *web* I spoke of above.)

Well, the best response to a lie is the truth. I want to describe below the truths that our cultural lies have displaced. I'm not trying to prove to you in this short letter (time to smile) that these are true; I only offer them to you as true.

Instead of *a web that traps and destroys us*, these truths form *a net that catches falling humans and saves us* from destruction by helping us understand ourselves and our Creator.

If Those Are Lies, What Is the Truth?

Truth #1. God does exist.

Not only does the God of the Bible exist, but He has revealed Himself to people—and He wants you to know Him and His will and purpose for your life.

God has revealed Himself to us in at least two ways:

1. He is revealed in what He has made (the physical universe), and

2. He has revealed Himself in His Word, the Bible.

Most people who have rejected the Bible as God's Word have not honestly examined the Bible's claims—they just accept what others have said about it.

Not only does God exist, not only has He revealed Himself, but He also wants to communicate His love for you—He wants to have a friendship relationship with you.

Now, just because you believe God exists does not mean that you have not been fooled into accepting some or all of these other cultural lies. Many people who say, "I believe in God," do not believe in the God of the Bible (they do not believe what God reveals about Himself in the Bible).

This truth of God's existence—and of Who He is and what He has done—establishes the next truth.

Truth #2. There are some absolute truths.

And that statement is one of them. Notice that the statement "There is no such thing as absolute truth" is self-refuting—the idea itself is stated as an absolute truth. (Time to smile again.) The fact that some "truths" are not universal does not alter the fact that some are.

The lie that there are no absolute truths has had a profound effect on ethics (morality). If there are no absolute truths, who is to say a behavior is wrong? If I receive great pleasure in torturing babies, who is to say I ought not do that? The lady who has been raped may label it as wrong, but the rapist found it exhilarating. It's all relative, right? Wrong.

This also touches on the idea that all religions are true and are paths that lead to the same God. The idea that all religions are equally right cannot be true, since many of them make contradictory or exclusionary claims.

We should not be surprised to discover that there is only one true religion. Many questions have only one right answer. What is the sum of 3 and 4? The correct answer—the only correct answer—is 7—all other answers are wrong.

Truth #3. Many things are as important as your happiness—maybe more important.

What could be more important than your happiness? How about feeding starving children, or stopping senseless murders, or preventing cruel rapes? Perhaps the entire world does not exist to bring you or me happiness.

Truth #4. Happiness is not the same as pleasure.

Our definition of happiness has changed over the last 50-100 years. When we are asked about our happiness, we often think in terms of immediate pleasure. Past generations included the ideas of honor, integrity, service to others, and fulfillment.

Consider the lives of the people who can afford every pleasure our culture has to offer. Are they happy? Very often they are not, and often these people admit that *pleasure* does not produce *happiness*. Most people would benefit from trying to accurately understand happiness.

Truth #5. Freedom does not produce happiness.

Unbridled freedom (acted out in your doing whatever comes to your mind) does not produce happiness—either in our lives or the lives of our family and loved ones. Some folks have been extremely happy even though they were wrongly imprisoned. Unbridled freedom produces guilt and chaos. And the next truth offers the reason for this.

Truth #6. God designed humans for a purpose.

The reason that the three previous statements (#3, #4, and #5 above) are true is found in this truth #6. Humans are not the result of a freak cosmic accident. God designed us—and He designed us for a purpose. So our only hope of genuine happiness—fulfillment and peace—in this life depends on our fulfilling the purposes for which God designed us.

Think of something you own that was designed for a purpose. Anything. A can-opener, a hammer, or a camera. You may be free to use your camera as a hammer, but you will have to pay the consequences. Using your hammer as a can-opener results in a mess. If you try to use your hammer as a camera, you'll get no pictures, and everyone will wonder if you have any common sense.

Similarly, only when our lives are lived within the boundaries of God's design can our lives have meaning and purpose. People who insist on exercising their freedom to live in a way contrary to God's design will pay the price, both in this life and the life to come. This is true for you and me too.

Truth #7. Every human life should have meaning and purpose.

The meaning of human life is connected to the value of human life. Two things address the value of human life. 1. God created humans in His likeness (no, you are not a god, and you are not just like God—but you bear His image). 2. God valued humans so highly that He sent His only son, Jesus, to die to pay for our sins. This determines the real value of any person.

Since God designed people for a purpose, we can hope to have a meaningful life if and only if we live according to God's design and purpose. And we cannot hope to find meaning in this life unless we discover this purpose.

God's laws (as recorded in the Bible) are not intended to suppress our freedom. Rather they are intended to show us the "design limits" the Creator built into us so that we can live "abundant" lives that are fulfilling, meaningful, and "happy."

Here is one example. Why does God tell us to enjoy sexual intimacy only with a husband or a wife? Because that is the way that He designed us. While we have the freedom to choose to live outside His design limits, we will suffer the consequences of our actions. If we choose homosexual freedom, we will pay the price for living outside God's design limits. I could repeat this many, many times—but I hope you get the point.

All of this brings me to address the claim that New Testament Christianity is the only true faith. I did not invent this claim. Jesus said it like this in John 14:6: "I am the way and the truth and the life. No one comes to the Father except through me." Sounds exclusive, huh? Other Bible passages reinforce this message, but my point is that anyone who claims to accept the Bible as God's Word is forced into embracing this position that Christianity is the only true religion.

Unfortunately, there are so many examples of fake Christianity and cultural Christianity, that many people doubt the existence of the real McCoy. If fakes exist, you better believe the genuine article also exists.

What is genuine, New Testament Christianity? Real Christianity centers on the person and work of Jesus of Nazareth. Jesus is the unique Son of God who lived a sinless life and died on the cross. If we place our faith in Him, then God will accept His death as payment (punishment) for our sins. If we refuse to place our faith in Him, then we will have to pay the penalty for our own sins—and that penalty is everlasting separation from God. So, you are free to choose.

As I said, the world (culture) you grew up in was radically different from the world that your father and I grew up in. We grew up in modernism, with its excessive confidence in human rationality. You grew up in a postmodern world that has much of this same excessive confidence in human rationality but is also willing to embrace mutually contradictory premises. If you like, at some time we might discuss more of the characteristics of our postmodern world, but I think this is enough for now.

Both of us (you and me) must learn to discover which parts of our culture are wrong but that shaped our worldviews—and reject them. We must also work to discover what truth is missing from our culture and embrace it. And this can take some time and could require some work—it sure has for me.

Our culture conditions us to embrace other lies too—this list is not complete. And though this letter is incomplete, I think it could serve as a great beginning! What do you think?

Your Friend,

Steve Badger

157

Prioritize These Doctrines

(Connect this to page 36.)

The gifts of the Holy Spirit	Water baptism by immersion
Christians must witness	The virgin birth of Jesus
The crucifixion of Jesus	The inerrancy of the Bible
Humans created in God's image	God exists as a Trinity
Original sin	The resurrection of Jesus
Salvation by grace, not by works	Christians must do good works
Christians not continuing in sin	Jesus is God's unique son
Sanctification	The immaculate conception
The infallibility of the Bible	The Apocrypha is not part of the Bible
Christians must read the Bible daily	Christians must observe the Lord's Supper
The Bible is our only authority	The age of accountability
God is the Creator	The role of women in the church
Predestination & freewill	Christians must attend church weekly
Length of hair on Christian men	God will judge everyone one day
Christians must pray daily	Angels
Satan	Heaven
Demons	The rapture of the saints
The KJV is the only Bible	Christians must pay tithes to the church
Length of hair on Christian women	The second coming of Christ
The initial physical evidence of the Holy Spirit baptism	Hell

158

An E-Tract on the Internet

(Connect this to page 57.)

What follows is a tract that I wrote as a witness and posted on my web site at http://steve-badger.net/publications/tract.html.

If "Christ is the Answer," What's the Question?

Steve Badger

Once several years ago, my brother and I were driving down the highway. I read aloud the car tag on the front of the car coming toward us: "Christ is the answer."

"If Christ is the answer," he responded, "what's the question?"

We smiled and thought we were pretty smart.

Today I realize that this car tag was right. Not only that, but I also know what the question is—or more correctly, what the questions are.

In a nutshell, Christ is the answer to all the questions of life.

But, the questions of life are not: Who was the 16th president of the US? Or, How long is the Mississippi River? Or, what is the value of π (pi) to 7 decimal places?

Then what are the questions of life like? They're a lot like these questions asked by thousands of people just like you every day:

◆ Who can take my loneliness away?
◆ What can I do about my overwhelming fear of dying?
◆ I was abused. Who can help me?
◆ What will restore my shattered marriage?
◆ How will I be able to care for my aged parents?
◆ My spouse has been unfaithful. What should I do?
◆ My son is on drugs. What will happen to him?
◆ We can't pay our bills, and we'll have to file for bankruptcy. Who will help?
◆ Where can I find direction in this confusing world?
◆ Where can I find the strength to overcome my destructive behavior habits?
◆ How will I ever save enough money for retirement?
◆ I have trouble sleeping and often have bad dreams. Where can I gain peace of mind?

- My wife needs medical help, but we cannot afford it. What can we do?
- My unmarried daughter is pregnant and considering an abortion. What should she do?
- My life has so little meaning, I'm thinking of ending my life. Does life have meaning?
- Who will help me build character and integrity in my children?
- Someone close to me has died. Will I survive my grief?

If any of these strikes a responsive chord, read on.

So, how can you make Christ the answer to the questions of your life?

1. Recognize that you need God's forgiveness. Why? Because we have all sinned.
2. Quit depending on your own abilities, turn to God, and ask Him to forgive you—on the basis of Jesus' death on the cross.
3. Put your trust in Christ Jesus as your savior and ruler.
4. Get involved with a group of others who are trying to do the same thing with their lives.

Christ is the answer. But He also provides answers to life's questions by directing you. One of the ways He will guide you is through the Bible. So if you don't have one, get a Bible and start reading it every day.

If you would like to make Christ Jesus the answer to the questions of your life, e-mail me and let's pray together on-line.

How Can a Natural Scientist Be a Christian Too?

By Steve Badger

(Connect this to page 63.)

Introduction

This is a very personal essay. In it I attempt to partially explain how a biochemist like me can be a conservative Christian and see the traditional, evangelical faith as rational. It is selective, brief, and arranged in neither chronological nor priority order.

Rarely does a person embrace a position for a single reason, and my Christian faith is probably no exception. Of necessity, this paper is not intended to be a complete or formal philosophical response to atheism. (For example, I do not address the problem of evil and suffering here.)

Of course, I could not remove from my memory the many influences that have shaped my thinking—and many of them are forgotten or their influence was subconscious; however, the writings of philosophers J.P. Moreland, L. Russell Bush, and Dallas Roark have recently influenced me.

I do not expect that the evidence that convinces me will necessarily convince you too. But I hope you will consider it with an open mind. ("Always be prepared to give an answer to everyone who asks you to give the reason for the hope that you have. But do this with gentleness and respect, keeping a clear conscience..." 1 Peter 3:15-16.)

Scientific Evidences

The physical universe

The most recent evidence indicates that the universe is finite in size and expanding. Though I do not necessarily subscribe to The Big Bang Theory of the origin of the universe, the fact that it at least appears similar to the biblical account of creation cannot be ignored. The physical universe seems to be finite in size and age. Beyond that, the universe appears to be "fine-tuned" to sustain life; that is, the fact that the universe is hospitable to life as we know it depends on the values of dozens of physical parameters being maintained within a very narrow range. This suggests Someone planned the universe and life for each other. ("For since the creation of the world God's invisible qualities—his eternal power and divine nature—have been clearly seen, being understood from what has been made, so that men are without excuse" Romans 1:20.)

The genetic material

When we discover information, we conclude intelligence produced it. If you saw "Mary loves Billy" inscribed in the sand at the beach, you would never conclude that waves had produced that message. You would scoff if a friend suggested the seagulls had written it. You would conclude that a person had written it. Could anyone convince you that random weather patterns carved the presidential likenesses on Mt. Rushmore? In a similar way, the enormous amount of information contained in the DNA of each species of life is overwhelming evidence for an Intelligent Designer. ("For God is not a God of disorder..." 1 Corinthians 14:33.)

Rational Reasons

The scientific method

Most of my undergraduate and graduate education are in the natural sciences. Most of my career has been based on using or teaching the natural sciences and its method. But in spite of these experiences, I have come to understand that the methods of science are neither infallible nor without limits. While the scientific method may be the best way to discover reality about physical phenomena, we could grant it exclusivity if and only if the physical realm is all that exists. Scientists are not the only ones who embrace the weight of the evidence. As a Christian, I think the weight of the evidence supports the reality of the Spirit God of the Bible. ("Since we are surrounded by such a great cloud of witnesses..." Hebrews 12:1.)

The Bible

I earned a B.S. in biology, completed the course work for an M.S. in microbiology, and earned a Ph.D. in chemistry. Then, 22 years after finishing a Ph.D., I earned my first master's degree—in biblical studies from a seminary. This seminary degree was completed about 23 years after I had become a Christian. After more than two decades of living the Christian life and reading and studying the Bible—including formal graduate studies—I am convinced that the Bible, including the New Testament, is reliable history. I find it rationally coherent. The message of the Bible builds my faith in God. For these reasons, I accept what it says. ("But these are written that you may believe that Jesus is the Christ, the Son of God, and that by believing you may have life in his name" John 20:31.)

Personal Experiences

The re-birth experience

Ultimately, becoming a Christian is not **merely** a rational decision—not that it is irrational. But in some sense it is arational, or, better yet, supra-rational. Though rational, it goes beyond reasoning. Genuine New Testament faith in Jesus as Messiah and Lord is first experiential. To that extent, it is subjective. But this subjectivity does not reduce it to a meaningless relativism. This experience has been the testimony of countless people through 20 centuries. ("In reply Jesus declared, 'I tell you the truth, no one can see the kingdom of God unless he is born again'" John 3:3.)

The Christian life

Space does not allow detailed account of God's transformation of my life, my family, and my mind since I placed my faith in Jesus. God's Spirit has transformed my way of living, my way of thinking, my way of relating to others. I've experienced his love, mercy, grace, and provision in countless ways. ("...If anyone is in Christ, he is a new creation; the old has gone, the new has come!" 2 Corinthians 5:17)

Contemporary Cultural Problems

I realize that many non-believers will hear my apologia and remain unconvinced. This may be due in part to our cultural baggage, and in this we are not unique. In New Testament times, Christianity was a scandal to the Jews because the Torah said, "anyone who is hung on a tree is under God's curse" (Deuteronomy 21:23). Thus,

163

they concluded, the crucifixion of Jesus proves he could not be God's Messiah. To the Greeks and Romans on the other hand, Christianity was a scandal because it failed to meet their philosophical tests of wisdom—especially the claims that Jesus had been raised from the dead. The Apostle Paul summed it up like this: "Jews demand miraculous signs and Greeks look for wisdom" (1 Corinthians 1:22).

Much of the cultural baggage of Westerners today also marshals against faith in Christ Jesus. Our Western culture is steeped in **relativism**. We are constantly told that there are no absolute truths—all truth is relative. Not only have many embraced relativism, but also they think it is especially true for all religious faith. "We're glad your Christian faith is true for you, but it is not equally true for all," they might tell Christians.

This relativism is married to our **pluralism**. To us, Christianity is a scandal because of its claims to exclusivity. This is such an overwhelming problem to many who profess the name of Christ, that they deny this claim that Jesus is the only path to God. I cannot agree with these Christians. C. S. Lewis (Professor of Medieval and Renaissance English Literature, Cambridge University, England) said it best in his book *Mere Christianity*:

> "I'm ready to accept Jesus as a great moral teacher, but I don't accept his claim to be God" [someone may say]. That is the one thing we must not say. A man who was merely a man and said the sort of things Jesus said would not be a great moral teacher. He would either be a lunatic—on a level with the man who says he is a poached egg—or else he would be the devil of Hell. You must take your choice. Either this man was, and is, the Son of God; or else a madman or something worse. You can shut him up for a fool, you can spit at Him and kill Him as a demon, or you can fall at His feet and call Him Lord and God. But let us not come with any patronizing nonsense about his being a great human teacher. He has not left that open to us. He did not intend to.

The claims of the world's competing religions cannot all be true—some are mutually exclusive. On the authority of Scripture we must assert the claims of Jesus: "I am the way and the truth and the life. No one comes to the Father except through me" (John 14:6).

Finally, we have allowed *science* to assume an authoritative preeminence. The scientific method may be the best method we've found to answer questions about the physical universe, but it is not without limits. And it is practiced by people who are as fallible, biased, and subjective as any other group of people. Too many people accept this scientific imperialism and falsely conclude that science has somehow demonstrated that God does not exist. Thus, too often Christians are marginalized in our world, and people who consider themselves educated are reluctant to consider seriously the faith claims of Christianity.

Challenge

Years ago I challenged a close friend who claimed agnosticism: "Read the New Testament with an open mind. I believe that God desires relationship with him more than you do. If the claims of Christianity are true, this God of the Bible is able to reveal himself to you in a way that you can accept him. I dare you to try it." He accepted that challenge and came to faith within a year. Do you dare accept that challenge? I hope so.

February 16, 2000

A Blessed Depression

By Steve Badger

[First published in *The Pentecostal Evangel*, Dec. 8, 1985.]

(Connect this to page 94.)

Dusk slowly turned the colors in my living room to shades of black and gray. The large old rental house was empty and depressingly silent. My wife and children had been out of town shopping all day and were not likely to return until late. My gloom intensified with the darkness.

My deepening depression was not merely loneliness but an accumulation of problems—scars of a recently changed sinful life-style. It was aggravated by guilt because of my inability to overcome my feelings.

I lay on our sofa, staring in the darkness at the 10-foot ceiling and praying for relief. Hot tears rolled out of my eyes, across my temples, and into my ears. My stomach ached; my body hurt. The effects of my mental depression were acutely physical.

God did not seem interested in my feelings of despair. Instead of comfort I felt His Spirit leading me to get up off my back and visit a non-Christian friend, Steve Quave. We were then in graduate school together.

Quave and I had been friends through most of graduate school. We had shared a sinful life-style, and he had watched—much closer than I had realized—as Jesus had turned my life right-side-up and started restoring my shattered 7-year-old marriage.

God was urging me to visit Quave, but I lay paralyzed with self-pity. I was angry because I felt no comfort from the Lord for my heaviness. All I could hear from Him was, "Get up and go visit Quave. Tell him of My love, power, and forgiveness. Tell him I love him."

Gradually my attitude changed from stubborn refusal to begrudging obedience.

I silently argued with God. "If I go, I'll tell him how I feel. I'm going to tell him just how down I've been. Don't expect me to cover up." The thought of having to argue with this Catholic-turned-agnostic scientist about "religion" aggravated my reluctance.

166

Couldn't God see I was in no condition to witness? Especially to Quave, who was even more imposing intellectually than he was physically. He had a strong, heavyset body and a quick, widely-read mind with an amazing memory and a knack for ferreting out faulty logic. I was in no shape to argue with him. It was just not the right time for me to witness to Quave. Couldn't God see that?

With a heart full of blues and a head full of wrong attitudes, I finally obeyed God and drove across town expecting to find his tiny apartment empty. Then I could complain even more to God about my frustrating life.

Quave was home and pleasantly surprised to see me. I had not been around him much since I had become a Christian, other than at school. For the first few minutes we chitchatted. Then Quave asked, "How are you doing?" meaning now that I was a Christian.

I fulfilled my threat. "Today...has been...the most depressing...day of my life." I spoke slowly with deep conviction.

His startled eyebrows raised. "I thought Christians didn't get depressed," he said. "I thought if you became a Christian, life was a bed of roses." He hadn't said this as an arrogant, easy cliché. He meant it.

"It hasn't been like that for me," I replied. "And I don't think that's what being a Christian is all about, anyway."

Instead of preventing a significant witness, this exchange provoked an animated, amicable discussion about what Christianity really is. He told me about his childhood in parochial schools, several concepts the priests and nuns had taught him, and what he thought Christianity was.

I had told him before how Jesus had changed my life, so now I gave him more details about what it meant for me to place my trust in God. I explained I was still trusting in Him during this time of general dissatisfaction with life.

As I left him that night, I felt sure Quave was no closer to finding God's salvation. My parting challenge was gentle, but direct: "Quave, read that modern English New Testament I gave you. As you read, pray this prayer: 'God—if there is a God—please reveal yourself to me as I read the Bible.'"

He looked reflective but gave no indication he would take my suggestion.

I had no sense of accomplishment as I left, but visiting my friend had lifted my spirits. As time passed, I grew in my faith and experienced depression less frequently, with less intensity, and for shorter periods of time.

Several months after that visit, Quave was born again. I was skeptical at first, but it was true. Christians and non-Christians alike were impressed with the way God saved this brilliant young man. His testimony glorified God and encouraged us.

A few years later and in another city, our close friendship was rekindled as we attended the same Assemblies of God church. More than once we thought how hilarious it would have been to us, back when we were deep in sin and far from God, if someone had told us that one day we would both be "fanatic Christians," worshipping together in a Pentecostal church and raising our hands and voices in praise to our Savior and God.

One night we rode home together after church and reminisced about how God had worked in our lives to save us. I asked him what he had thought the night I had visited him during my bout of wretched depression. I could not believe my ears! He did not remember my depression or his "bed of roses" comment!

Instead Quave remembered he had been alone and lonely, and I had visited him. He had been feeling unloved and wishing someone would come see him, and I had knocked on his door! God had used Quave's feelings to make him receptive to me and my witness. And God used me in spite of me.

My vision blurred as I recounted my unhappiness of that night. He again failed to recall it. Then his eyes filled with tears as he thanked me for loving him enough to come over and talk with him. I felt so undeserving of his appreciation as we thanked God together in prayer.

My friend then shared something with me that I had not known: that night was the beginning of his months-long odyssey culminating in new life in Christ. That night had been pivotal in his life. And I had almost missed it!

A few years later God answered one of Quave's most important prayers by providing him with a Christian wife. Within a few years they had children, two boys.

One night in early 1982 when I was out of town on business, I had an emergency phone call from my wife: Quave had been killed instantly in an auto accident.

I returned to my room with a Christian friend to kneel together and cry and pray. Part of my prayer was simply, "God, thanks for getting me out of my self-pity that night to tell Quave of Your Love. Thank You, Jesus."

An Online Personal Testimony

(Connect this to page 97.)

God's Amazing Grace: A Personal Testimony

By Steve Badger

http://steve-badger.net/misc/testmony.html

I grew up as the youngest of five children, with Christian parents who lived out their faith in God. We were not Pentecostal, but conservative, mainline evangelicals. Daily family devotions included prayer and Scripture readings, and by the time I was a teenager I had read through the Bible more than once.

I was about 7-years-old when I first professed faith in Jesus as Savior. I'm sure I understood much of what I was doing, but I was a young child with mixed motives. But I felt secure that I was eternally saved.

By the time I finished high school, I was not trying to obey the Lord but was living a worldly lifestyle. Almost every time I went to church I could feel God's Spirit drawing me to Himself, but I consistently determined to wait. I silently said I should wait until I married, or until I finished college, or until our first baby was born.

Thus I found myself in graduate school, married with one child, and far from God though fairly regular in church attendance. My father and Ed, a friend at the university, conspired behind my back to pray for my salvation. Within months Ed found an opportunity to talk with me about my faith in God.

Late one night Ed just happened to bump into me as I worked preparing materials to teach a lab the next day. He started asking me about my faith, making me feel very uncomfortable, of course. Most of the answers I gave Ed included quoting or paraphrasing a passage of the Bible.

Then Ed asked me to try to summarize what being a Christian meant. "Jesus said that if any man wanted to follow Him, he would have to take up his cross."

"And what does it mean to take up your cross?" Ed asked.

After a brief hesitation I answered, "I guess He was speaking of the burdens we must all bear in life."

But Ed pressed on, "The cross was a burden, but that's not the central meaning. You see, after they hung the cross on the Christ, they hung the Christ on the cross!" I wasn't really following his argument, but he continued, "The cross was an instrument of execution, of death, for Jesus. He was saying, 'If you want to follow me, you must die.'"

This sounded pretty radical to me. I sure didn't want to die any time soon. But Ed kept on explaining. "Who is the King of your life? You are. You are sitting on the throne of your life as the ruler. And Jesus is still nailed to the cross as far as you are concerned. But He wants you to get off the throne, take Him off the cross, and put Him on the throne of your life as your Ruler. If you do that, the only position left for you is the cross. Your will must be put to death so that His will can reign in you. And when this happens, you will be born again."

We discussed these things for a while, then I left to drive the 20-odd miles home. But God's Spirit went to work in my heart and mind, bringing to consciousness some of the Scriptures I had learned as a child.

As I drove north on the interstate a little faster than the speed limit allowed, the Holy Spirit dealt with me. Without warning I began praying aloud. "Wow, God! That's right!" That was my whole prayer, but it summed up my acceptance of the Gospel message Ed had shared with me. And when I prayed, something new, unique, wonderful-yet-frightening happened to me. Please bear with me as I try to describe it. There was so much light, I could not see. There was so much beautiful sound, I could not hear. The air smelled wonderful! Even my skin was being stimulated by something. My senses were short-circuited.

How could I drive? I have no idea. But I immediately knew Who had just entered the car. He was Jesus, and I now knew by experience that Jesus was alive. And some time later I realized that I was sitting in my car, parked in my driveway, and I had no idea how I got there.

Most would think that after such an awesome experience, I would simply grow in my new faith. Instead, I lived for the Lord for just a few months, and then gradually slipped into all of my old patterns of trusting and living for myself. Then I fell into sins I had never committed before.

By this time I had about a year-and-a-half left to finish my doctorate in chemistry, and my wife and I had two children, a son and a daughter. And my wife and I were in the process of seeking a divorce as a result of a sinful lifestyle.

To help me dissolve my marriage, I planned to quit graduate school and move to another city. I had accepted a job in a nearby major metropolitan area and was driving toward this city, when I unexpectedly prayed aloud. "God, I know this is not Your will for me. But right now this is more important to me. After I finish this, I will come back to You and let You work out another will for my life." What arrogance! To think that I could dictate to God! Our gracious God did not end my life right then and there, but before sunset that day He brought all of my plans to an end. That evening I drove back home and continued my education. But my life was most miserable as I suffered a deep and prolonged depression.

Soon after that, God, in His grace, sent another to witness to me. Another friend, George, came to tell me of his search for God. Since I didn't have time during the day to talk with George, we made arrangements to meet at John's house that evening.

John, his wife, Pete, and I all sat around John's living room listening to a wonderful story of God's miraculous *coincidences* to provide George with the witness he needed. But I didn't get to hear the story that first time.

As I sat there on the couch, God's Spirit spoke in my mind. "Do you remember the commitment you made to Me?" he asked. Of course I did. "I have been calling you, but you have not been hearing me," He continued. God now had my undivided attention, and I was terrified! "Why have you been ignoring Me? You go to church, but you ignore Me!"

I'm sure I thought out my excuses, but God ignored them as he continued, "I have been calling you for a long time, and you have not answered. This will be the last time you will hear me call you if you do not answer now. Will you come and follow me? Will you let Me rule your life?" His questions demanded an answer, an immediate answer.

"I hope I don't freak anyone out," I blurted out to my friends, "but I have to pray."

George suggested, "I'm almost through with my story, if you want to wait to pray then." Story? George had been telling us a story? I hadn't really noticed.

"I'm sorry, I have to pray right now," I answered. And I turned and knelt at that couch and very quietly whispered, "God, I do hear You now, and I will follow You now. Please do not leave me." After a few more minutes of prayer I turned and sat up on the couch again. And later I had George tell his story again so that I could hear it too.

This occurred after Thanksgiving, and two very important things happened before Christmas. I was baptized in the Holy Spirit—in spite of the fact that I had never had any real interaction with Pentecostal Christians. And my wife recommitted her life to the Lord, then we committed our marriage to the Lord.

My old friends were shocked at my radically changed lifestyle. "Don't worry," they reassured me, "within a few weeks you'll be back with us doing the things we do. This Jesus-freak stuff is just a phase that will soon pass."

That was over 30 years ago, and it hasn't passed yet. And I expect it never will.

Exercises to Develop Strategy

(Connect this to pages 40 and 123.)

In your journal try to outline an initial approach (strategy) that you might take to witness to each of the following people. Assume that you have been developing a friendship with this person and have gained a level of trust that would allow you to begin asking questions and sharing personal experiences.

Don't go into too much detail here—just try to outline one or more possible approaches. Write out any assumptions that you wish to add to the description provided. Also, list the things that you would like to learn about this person before you share too much of your own faith journey.

If you are in a group, your discussion leader is not going to give you "the right answers." But discussing these in the group could help you learn how to arrive at strategies that will help you witness.

1. Chris is a college student who grew up in an evangelical church, but seemed to abandon his parents' faith when he went to college. "I guess I just out-grew God," he told you once. "I don't need my parents' religion." He's not living a grossly immoral life, but he shuns everything Christian. You and he are roommates. (Ladies, change *he* to *she* and *his* to *her*.)

2. Lisa is 36 and a single mother. She has no immediate family living nearby and works long hours to support herself and her 9-year-old daughter. She has just been diagnosed with an illness that is likely to end her life within two or three years, and she knows it. Her life is one crisis after another.

3. Tom is your age and a co-worker on your job. You have been planing to witness to him. You've never had any job related problems with him, and you are fairly close friends, but only on the job. Yesterday Tom told everyone that he is homosexual and living with his lover. He has no church background.

4. You and Stephanie went to high school together, but never knew each other very well. She is a 21-year-old who often struggles with depression. You've been told that she has had an abortion—

maybe even two. She lives a promiscuous life and drinks to excess at parties most weekends. For some reason, she likes you (only as a friend) and seems to respect your life and opinions.

5. Ken and Fran have just moved into the house (apartment) next to you. You learn that they are not married, but they've been living together for four or five years. They have no children. You know that they go to church somewhere occasionally.

6. Bill is a divorcee who goes to your church rather faithfully, but you've seen enough of his life to doubt his faith walk. In fact, you suspect he is going to church only to find a mate.

7. Your new next-door neighbors are Buddhists from Eastern Asia (or Hindus from Southern Asia, or Moslems from the Middle East). Their ethnic and linguistic background is radically different from yours, but their children are close to the ages of your children.

Glossary

Agnostic - doubts a person can know whether or not God exists.

Anthropology - The scientific study of the origin, the behavior, and the physical, social, and cultural development of human beings. Anthropology differs from other social sciences (e.g. psychology, sociology) in that it relies heavily on data gathered by observing non-literate peoples and from archaeology. Described as a "unifying science," anthropology incorporates biology, geology, linguistics, psychology, and archaeology. The field is roughly divided into two major disciplines: 1) physical anthropology and 2) cultural anthropology

Apologetic - a formal defense of a position

Cognitive dissonance – embracing two contradictory ideas as true

Contextualization – in the best sense, explaining the Gospel in terms of the recipient's culture

Culture - The totality of socially transmitted behavior patterns, arts, beliefs, institutions, and all other products of human work and thought

Deconstruction – "The postmodern literary discipline of uncovering the opposing ideas implied in a text and demonstrating how the author has favored one side over the other because of his or her social context. Demonstrating how texts' truth claims defeat themselves" [96]

Doctrine - a teaching; something taught

Empiricism – claims experience is the only source of knowledge

Enlightenment, The – modern thought originated in Europe during the 17th and 18th centuries with the works of Locke, Voltaire, Hume, Rousseau, Kant, Pascal, Bacon, Newton; this period is called "The Enlightenment," and human reasoning came to be considered supreme

---

[96] Quoted from the glossary (p.281) in McCallum's *the Death of Truth*.

Epistemology - branch of philosophy that deals with knowledge, attempting to answer these questions: How do we know? What do we mean when we say we know something?

Ethics – the study of morals, of what persons ought and ought not do

Exegesis – critical analysis of a written text; sometimes used as a synonym for hermeneutics

False dichotomy – offering two choices, thus implying one of them is right and masking the fact that the right choice is actually a third choice that has not been mentioned

Hermeneutics – a study of the principles of the exegesis and interpretation of a text; the adjective is hermeneutical

Homiletics – the study of the creation and proclamation of a sermon

Humanism – a religion that denies the existence of God while claiming that humans can solve all of their own problems

Incommensurable – having no common standard of comparison, thus, not able to be compared

Law of non-contradiction – a statement and its negation cannot both be simultaneously true; A cannot be non-A at the same time and in the same sense

Metanarrative - used by postmodernists as a pejorative for a worldview

Modernism – characterized by an excessive confidence in human reason to solve the problems that plague humans; modernism resulted from The Enlightenment

Objective - the conclusion does not depend on the person making the observation

Pejorative - A belittling or insulting word or expression; often the word itself is not insulting, but the tone of voice makes it a put-down

Pluralism - used in a variety of ways: can be used 1. to indicate the (ethnic) diversity in a culture; or 2. to claim that the truth claims of all subcultures are equally valid

Postmodernism – re-read the first two chapters of this book

Pragmatism - whatever works is truth; "you cannot argue with success"

Qumran community – an isolated, apocalyptic Jewish sect that was very critical of the Jews in power, i.e. the ones at Jerusalem; they had a distinctive understanding of the Jewish sacred writings; they existed during the time of Christ and were destroyed by the Romans in A.D. 68

Relativism - the idea that a group determines what concepts are true; thus, what is true for me may not be true for you

Sanctification – the process of our character traits being changed into the character traits of Jesus

Science - a method of gaining knowledge about the physical world; the method does not lend itself to answering ethical questions (right and wrong)

Scientism - a philosophy based on a faith that the physical realm is all there is; thus the methods of natural science are our only hope of gaining reliable knowledge

Subjective - the conclusion depends on the person making the observation

Syncretism - a fusion of two or more differing belief systems

Worldview - The overall perspective from which one sees and interprets the world. Translation of the German word *Weltanschauung.*

Useful Web Sites

Please understand that the Internet is extremely dynamic. You might find a web site one day and not the next. These links were good the last time I looked. If you cannot find them, you might try searching using the name of the author and some of the key words in the title.

Author, Title	URL: http://
Jim Leffel, "The New Challenge: Christian Apologetics"	http://www.xenos.org/ministries/crossroads/cornel1.htm
Jim Leffel, "Christian Witness in a Pluralistic Age "	www.xenos.org/essays/pluralsm.htm
Jim Leffel, "Postmodernism: The 'Spirit of the Age'"	www.xenos.org/essays/relrev2.htm
Gene E. Veith, "Postmodern Times: Facing a World of New Challenges & Opportunities"	www.capo.org/premise/95/sep/p950807.html
Graeme Codrington, "Generation X Papers: Methods of Evangelistic Contact"	www.youth.co.za/papers/yevangel.htm
Anon., "Postmodernism and You"	www.xenos.org/ministries/crossroads/pmandyou.htm
Dennis McCallum, "Are We Ready?"	www.xenos.org/ministries/crossroads/dotch1.htm
Anon., "Christian Tradition, Post-modern Worldview and Evangelism."	www.churcharmy.com.au/E3.htm

Apologetics web sites:

Web site	URL: http://
Stand to Reason	www.str.org/
Barna Research On-line	www.barna.org/
Biblical Studies Foundation	http://www.bible.org/

The Internet is extremely dynamic—information found at a particular site today may not be there tomorrow. I have paper and electronic copies of all Internet articles that I've referenced.

Bibliography

Apologetics

Carlson, Richard F. *Science and Christianity: Four Views.* InterVarsity Press, 2000.

Kennedy, Rick. *Faith at State: A Handbook for Christians at Secular Universities,* InterVarsity Press, 1995.

Lewis. C. S. *Mere Christianity.* Macmillan Publishing Co., 1943, 1945, 1952.

McGrath, Alister E. *Intellectuals Don't Need God and Other Modern Myths.* Zondervan, 1993.

Phillips, Timothy R. and Dennis L. Okholm. *Christian Apologetics in the Postmodern World.* InterVarsity Press, 1995.

Sire, James W. *Why Should Anyone Believe Anything at All?* InterVarsity Press, 1994.

Witnessing & Evangelism

Barna, George. *Evangelism that Works: How to Reach Changing Generations with the Unchanging Gospel,* Regal Books, 1995.

Careaga, Andrew. *E-vangelism: Sharing the Gospel in Cyberspace,* Vital Issues Press, 1999.

Carson, D. A. Editor. *Telling the Truth: Evangelizing Postmoderns.* Zondervan, 2000.

Ford, Kevin Graham. *Jesus for a New Generation.* InterVarsity Press, 1995.

Hunter, Jr., George E. *How to Reach Scular People.* Abingdon Press, 1992.

Hybels, Bill, and Mark Mittelberg. *Becoming a Contagious Christian.* Zondervan, 1994.

Johnson, Ronald W. *How Will They Hear If We Don't Listen?* Broadman & Holman Publishers, 1994.

Long, Jimmy. *Generating Hope.* InterVarsity Press, 1997.

MacArthur, Jr., John F. *Nothing But the Truth: Upholding the Gospel in a Doubting Age.* Crossway Books, 1999.

Nash, Ronald H. *Worldviews in Conflict.* Zondervan, 1992.

Pollard, Nick. *Evangelism Made Slightly Less Difficult: How to Interest People Who Aren't Interested.* InterVarsity Press, 1997.

Roxburgh, Allan J. *Reaching a New Generation.* InterVarsity Press, 1993.

Scifres, Mary J. *Searching for Seekers.* Abingdon Press, 1998.

Strobel, Lee. *Inside the Mind of Unchurched Harry & Mary: How to Reach Friends and Family Who Avoid God and the Church.* Zondervan, 1993.

Van Pelt, Nancy. *Creative Hospitality: How to Turn Home Entertaining into a Real Ministry.* Review and Herald Pub. Association, 1995.

Postmodernism

Anderson, Kenton. *Preaching with Conviction: Connecting with Postmodern Listeners.* Kregel Publications, 2001.

Allen, Diogenes. *Christian Belief in a Postmodern World.* Westminster/John Knox, 1989.

Beckwith, Francis J. and Gregory Koukl. *Relativism: Feet Firmly Planted in Mid-Air.* Baker Books, 1998.

Carson, D. A. *The Gagging of God.* Zondervan, 1996.

Dockery, David S. Editor, *The Challenge of Postmodernism.* Baker, 1995.

Grenz, Stanley. *A Primer on Postmodernism.* Eerdmans, 1996.

Groothuis, Douglas. *Truth Decay.* InterVarsity Press, 2000.

Henderson, David W. *Culture Shift.* Baker Books, 1998.

Hicks, Rick and Kathy Hicks. *Boomers, Xers, and Other Strangers.* Tyndale House, 1999.

Johnston, Graham. *Preaching to a Postmodern World: A Guide to Reaching Twenty-first Century Listeners.* Baker, 2001.

Kallenberg, Brad. *Live to Tell: Evangelism for a Postmodern Age.* Brazos Press, 2002.

Kelly, Gerrard. *Retrofuture: Rediscovering Our Roots, Recharting Our Routes.* InterVarsity.Press, 1999.

McCallum, Dennis, editor. *The Death of Truth.* Bethany House, 1996.

McLaren, Brian. *More Ready Than You Realize: Evangelism as Dance in the Postmodern Matrix.* Zondervan, 2002.

Palmer, Michael D., ed. *Elements of a Christian Worldview.* Logion Press, 1998.

Phillips, Timothy R. and Dennis L. Okholm. *Christian Apologetics in the Postmodern World.* InterVarsity Press 1995.

Sweet, Leonard. *AquaChurch.* Group Pub., 1999.

_____. *SoulTsunami: Sink or Swim in New Millennium Culture.* Zondervan, 1999.

Veith, Gene Edward. *Postmodern Times.* Crossway Books, 1994.

Faith and Reason

Miethe, Terry L. *A Christian's Guide to Faith & Reason.* Bethany House Publishers, 1987.

Moreland, J. P. *Love your God with All Your Mind: The Role of Reason in the Life of the Soul.* NavPress, 1997.

Nash, Ronald H. *Faith and Reason: Searching for a Rational Faith.* Zondervan, 1988.

Veith, Gene Edward. *Loving God with All Your Mind: How to Survive and Prosper as a Christian in the Secular University and Post-Christian Culture.* Crossway Books, 1987.

About the Author

Steve Badger is a Professor of Chemistry at Evangel University in Springfield, Missouri. With a B.S. in biology and a Ph.D. in biochemistry and microbiology, he has taught in Christian colleges and state colleges and universities, worked in a privately owned environmental testing laboratory, done research in government research labs, and served as a consultant.

As an ordained Assemblies of God minister, he served as a senior pastor for five years and as an associate pastor for several more years. He has also preached and/or taught in Mexico, the People's Republic of the Congo, Bulgaria, South Africa, Kenya, England, and the Dominican Republic—as well as dozens of places across the USA. He has written several articles published in *Advance, Pentecostal Evangel, Today's Man, Insight for Young Adults*, and *Paraclete* (all Assemblies of God publications).

In 1995, Dr. Badger earned an M.A. in Biblical Literature at the Assemblies of God Theological Seminary—22 years after completing his Ph.D. He has also been involved in training college professors and ministers to use computers and the Internet for religious studies research. You can visit his website at www.steve-badger.net.

Steve and his wife, Dale, enjoy Thai food, watching nature shows, and visiting their two adult daughters.